THE POST CHARISMATIC EXPERIENCE

The New Wave of the Spirit

Rev. Robert A. Wild

LIVING FLAME PRESS
BOX 74 LOCUST VALLEY, N.Y. 11560

Cover: Robert Manning

Scripture quotations are from the New American Bible

Published by: Living Flame Press/Box 74/Locust Valley, New York 11560.

ISBN: 0-914544-50-0

Printed in the United States of America.

Dedication

To Catherine de Hueck Doherty who helped me
to understand and live more deeply the mystery
of Nazareth.

Foreword

This book presupposes a great deal of acquaintance with the charismatic renewal in the churches. I am concerned here primarily with the large group of people who, in many ways, have passed through the formal renewal, or charismatic movement. Despite this particular focus, it is hoped that all Christians will find something of value in these pages.

I believe that there is a positive dimension to the phenomenon of people no longer involved in the charismatic movement. The book, therefore, is an attempt to give an interpretation of something already happening and does not presume, at this early stage of the phenomenon, to have definitive answers. Rather, it is an exploratory book, seeking to understand what the Spirit is saying to the churches. It is offered in a spirit of openness, to further the dialogue on this phenomenon of people "passing through" the charismatic movement.

It risks being misunderstood from a variety of angles. Some in the charismatic movement may tend to see the book as an attack on the charismatic movement and therefore as "dangerous." Some may interpret me as saying that post-charismatics are "more advanced" and/or better than charismatics. Some may think that I am whitewashing the defects of those who have withdrawn. Some who have left the charismatic movement for the wrong reasons may see it as a confirmation of their lack of generosity. And, despite all my efforts, perhaps many will understand "post-charismatic" to mean those who no longer believe in or live out what the Spirit has taught them in the renewal.

I accept all these risks because I believe the truth at stake is important enough. Basically, what I hope to do is give some insights to people who have indeed been led by the Spirit into other avenues of their spiritual lives, after their participation in the charismatic movement.

Finally, I know it will be said, "Oh no, not another label! Now we have post-charismatics too!" I'm afraid we can't do without labels if we are going to try to articulate reality – which we must do. My prayer is that we will remember we are all brothers and sisters in the same family, and that we will not lose our sense of humor!

Madonna House
Combermere, Ontario

Contents

Foreword		7
1.	Who are Post-Charismatics?	9
2.	Enthusiasm in the Spirit: Ten Years After	22
3.	The Return to Nazareth	41
4.	Heading Across the Desert	65
5.	Love Beyond Everything	82
6.	Winning the World for Christ	96
7.	Refocus on the Church	111
Afterword		126
Footnotes		128

One

Who are Post-Charismatics?

Over the past four or five years the leaders in the charismatic movement have been grappling with the phenomenon of people "dropping out" of the formal renewal movement. What does this "dropping out" mean? Is it good or bad? A work of the Spirit, or not? I would like briefly to present the evolution of thinking on this question of one of the leaders in the renewal, Kevin Ranaghan, as a way of situating the theme and purpose of this book. In an early article in *New Covenant* entitled, "Has the Charismatic Renewal Peaked?" (April, 1980), he concluded by saying: "Thus, as the renewal enters the eighties, we need to re-examine the record of our performance, to seek fresh vision and direction from the Lord, and to make the necessary adjustments and corrections in our lives and services" (p. 19). It was after I read that article that most of this book, which is something of the vision and direction the Lord gave to *me,* was written.

In this above-mentioned article, Ranaghan describes the present situation through statistics regarding prayer groups, Life in the Spirit seminars, attendance at conventions, and subscriptions to *New Covenant*. His interpretation of the "dropping out" problem was that there was a "revolving door phenomenon" at work:

Tens of thousands of Catholics continue to be baptized in the Holy Spirit each year, but the number of known prayer groups and size of known prayer groups show little growth. There must be hundreds of thousands of Catholics baptized in the Holy Spirit who do not go to prayer meetings. Of these, tens of thousands have, after some period of involvement, dropped out of the prayer meetings. The drop-off of older members and the increase of new members, as well as the disbanding of old prayer groups and the starting up of new prayer groups, cancel each other out. . . .the charismatic renewal has not peaked, though it has come to a plateau.

At that time, in 1980, he asked leaders and participants what they thought were the reasons for this state of affairs. They listed all *negative* reasons – lack of leadership, individualism, conflicts in prayer groups, and so on.

In a follow-up article on the same subject in the same year (*New Covenant*, June, 1980), Ranaghan said that "most leaders in the Catholic charismatic renewal with whom (he) had spoken agreed that the revolving door phenomenon [by which he meant people entering the renewal and then simply returning to their former situations] was a result of "misguided or sinful efforts of either leaders or participants or both." He concluded: "The revolving door does not, on the whole, seem to be God's will" (p. 21).

What amazed me most about this interpretation was the absence of any really positive, legitimate reasons for withdrawal from the formal charismatic movement. Surely there are some valid reasons, inspired by the Spirit himself, why some people—perhaps many—have passed through the movement and no longer attend prayer meetings, or are involved formally in things charismatic. At that time I believed there was a positive dimension to the peaking question which needed to be explored more deeply.

In that June article, Ranaghan did give the opinion of a bishop:

> One possible explanation for the revolving door was recently given to me by a bishop. Many people, he suggested, go through the renewal and experience significant personal renewal in the Lord. But they experience the renewal with its prayer groups and conferences as a training camp or staging ground, and after a while they move, renewed and gifted, into the flow of wider church life. They become involved in parish and diocesan institutions and programs, and services. Finding their places there, they both benefit and are benefited by the local church. They give much valuable service, and receive ongoing formation and nourishment from the normal services of the local church. This, the bishop thought, was a good thing both for the renewal and for the diocese. He did not know how widespread this scenario might be, though it seemed to apply to his experience. (p. 20).

Ranaghan commented that this explanation "may be accurate in some places."

A survey conducted that same year by the Religious News Service ("Shift Seen in Charismatic Activities," *Courier Journal,* May 7, 1980), indicated that the bishop's opinion was accurate in more than some places:

A Religious News survey of renewal leaders brought back a virtually unanimous response – what is happening is not so much a decrease in numbers but a diversification of activities for those who came into the movement in the past decade.

. . .many are apparently exercising their Christian ministries within more traditional structures.

Father Robert Hargraves . . . Cumberland, R.I.: 'Many people have gone through a stage where they felt they needed prayer meetings and now are moving into other ministries. I see more people talking about the Lord at their jobs, with their friends and in their families . . . like a child with a new toy, we were attracted by the glitter (of the renewal), but we soon came to realize it was an occasion for us to grow spiritually and to move to a deeper level.'

Robert Turbitt, Coventry, R.I.: 'I have never met anyone yet who was a charismatic and then decided that he or she is no longer a charismatic.'

Dan Malachuk, *Logos Journal*: 'There's a great infiltration into the system . . . charismatics have begun to operate as persuaders rather than evangelicals within the system.'

Even in 1980, this positive aspect of the "dropping out" phenomenon was present. I believe it has continued to grow and is now present on a large scale. In a very recent article ("Charismatic Movement and Charismatic Renewal," *New Covenant,* June, 1983), Ranaghan confirms that there is a large-scale, positive dimension to the "dropping out" phenomenon:

> . . .observation both inside and outside the charismatic renewal reveals that large numbers of Catholics who were once active in the charismatic movement have left the activities and structures of the movement behind in order to invest themselves in other forms of ministry and service in the church.
>
> They come into these new areas of service baptized in the Holy Spirit, tempered by the fires of Pentecost, and equipped both with zeal and with spiritual gifts for serving others.

I would agree that these people have dropped out. But I would not agree that those who have been nurtured, renewed, and strengthened in the charismatic movement and who then are led into new areas of service in the church fit that definition. Moving on is definitely not dropping out.

He concludes the article by making a distinction between the charismatic renewal and the charismatic renewal movement. "The charismatic renewal embraces all those men, women, and children . . . who have been baptized in the Holy Spirit and who are being led by God into a deeper life of worship, holiness, service, and love. They may or may not be involved in a movement." "The charismatic renewal movement, on the other hand, is the total of all the individuals, groups, and activities that foster the charismatic renewal in the church at large. The movement does not have to be as large as the renewal" (*New Covenant*, June, 1983).

In an article in *Review For Religious* (March/April, 1982) I spoke of the "post-charismatic phenomenon," and used the word "post-charismatics." My intention in using this word is not to coin a new technical term of some kind. It is simply my convenient way of speaking about these people who have passed through the movement; it should not be taken too seriously as a label. It roughly coincides with what Ranaghan now calls the charismatic renewal. I say "roughly" because "charismatic renewal" seems to imply people still using the charismatic gifts, only now outside the movement. Some of this is happening. What I think is happening on a wider scale, however, is the phenomenon of people being led into kinds of spiritualities where the gifts are not evident, or not being exercised in ways they are exercised in the movement. It is this latter phenomenon especially I call "post-charismatic."

What is becoming clearer is that we are not dealing with a revolving door but simply with a door. The former image implies that people enter, and then are spun around and shot back to where they came from. The revolving door image seems to imply that people are not getting out at the other end. I think it is clear now that many people are passing through the charismatic renewal movement (to use Ranaghan's distinction) into the wider stream of the Church's spiritualities.

Where have they gone? What are they doing? Why have they withdrawn? In lieu of a questionnaire to these people (which might not be a bad idea), I base my interpretation on my own personal experience, and on personal encounters with many, many people. My interpretation is positive: the Spirit is leading many people into deeper life. This is what I see happening, and it is also my *hope.*

It is my hope because I believe the charismatic movement is a work of the Spirit and that the work of the Spirit endures in peoples' hearts. Some have left the renewal altogether and gone back to their "old ways." This is certainly a part of any movement of such size. Some may have left the movement because of defects, problems encountered, etc. Still others may wish to be in the movement, but unavoidable circumstances prevent them from doing so. My interpretation is, however, that a great many people are being moved by the Spirit into other expressions of their life with God. Some may know what is happening; others may not have too much reflective awareness. My hope in this book is to provide some of that awareness.

Ranaghan has defined the renewal as "all those who have been baptized in the Holy Spirit and who are being led by God into a deeper life." It seems to me there are three main types now within the renewal, with many variations. First are those in the movement; second are those outside the movement who look to the movement for their guidance and spirituality; third, those who are being led into other spiritualities, where the gifts are exercised in ways uncharacteristic of the movement. The book is concerned primarily with those in this last category, although I hope it will have something to say to all Christians and to all in the renewal. "Post-charismatic" refers especially to new ways of expressing and living the charisms – ways less stereotyped, ways more integrated with other traditional spiritualities and ordinary daily life. Post-charismatics are not people who have left the riches of the renewal. The riches of the renewal have led them to other riches.

In actual life, of course, the above distinctions may often be blurred. Post-charismatics who have interiorized the gifts may occasionally frequent prayer meetings, or use their gifts in the movement when the Spirit bids them do so. But generally, these people are now finding their spiritual nourishment and mission elsewhere. After some years of involvement in the movement, they have felt a need for a rethinking, a re-evaluation, of their life in the Spirit. For many, this re-evaluation has led to a new stage of growth in the Spirit. I will dwell, therefore, on some of the positive reasons why people are choosing to move into this post-charismatic stage of the renewal. Thousands of people have chosen to live the life of the Spirit in more hidden, less obvious ways.

While designating some people in the renewal as post-charismatic, I think it would be misleading to speak of a post-charismatic age, possibly even harmful to do so. The Spirit has reminded us that the powerful exercise of the charismatic gifts should always have a definite and permanent place within the Church. Ranaghan speaks of "those who have been called by God to work in the charismatic renewal movement and to foster charismatic renewal in the whole church." If this explicit charismatic dimension was ever in danger of being lost again or forgotten, I think it would be the Lord's will for people to become involved in a movement again. At the present time, there seems little danger that the movement will cease. It is my own prayerful opinion that it should *not* cease.

I do not really agree with the oft-repeated phrase, the "receding wave of the renewal." I do not believe in any real way that the renewal is receding. It is very much alive, if we see it in the broad spectrum of the three groups I outlined above. The wave of the Spirit is continuing to rise in many hidden ways. But I think many people will not continue to grow, nor the movement understand its specific place in the Church, unless it is understood and accepted that the Lord can call people to other spiritual paths within and through the renewal.

Many people need and deserve to hear it said to them: "Yes, it's all right. Go ahead. Your movement away from a specific charismatic spirituality has a place in our traditional Christian heritage. It is perfectly true that you may be called to new paths in your walk with God. Don't feel guilty, or that you are dropping out. Continue to follow the Spirit in your heart."

One reason why many people are confused and hesitant about these new pathways is that the charismatic movement is seen too much as the prime analogue to which everything must be referred. Sometimes this impression is given. The gospel is the only prime analogue. And there are many kinds of gospel expressions, many kinds of spiritualities in the Church, many kinds of mysticisms. We must be ready to revise our positions when the Spirit moves. "The Spirit blows where he wills." "The Spirit breaks down old patterns and creates new life." "The Spirit is a-movin all over this land." Such phrases were common at the beginning of the movement. Can they not still apply to the whole of the renewal?

If tens of thousands of people have passed through the movement, and if thousands of new people continue to join, then the movement is doing an incredibly wonderful job! The Religious News Service I quoted above also cited a Gallup Poll taken in 1980 "which revealed that there are 29 million charismatics in the United States today—19 percent of the total population." What a cause for rejoicing and for praising God!

It simply needs to be admitted now that for very many people the movement will be a door through which they pass along the Spirit's specific path for each of them. It has been said for years that the goal of the renewal is to cease as a movement and to become integrated into the rest of the life of the Church. I think it is clear now that the renewal is becoming integrated into the life of the Church in ways that were not initially conceived; the movement has become integrated as well, but as a movement, as an explicit, specific form of spirituality. Perhaps the movement should no longer be called a movement, but seen as this specific charismatic spirituality which forms a permanent part of the Church's life.

I think we should be much more optimistic and hopeful about the direction of the renewal. Departures from the movement may well be a real sign of vitality and not a cause for alarm at all. What should be a cause for concern is whether or not these people will find the spiritual nourishment and guidance they need. The movement probably is not called to provide this further guidance, because the individual paths and needs are becoming too diverse. Trying to provide such comprehensive guidance may well divert the movement from its main task.

The movement should not feel responsible for the whole spiritual journey. Some of the soul-searching in this area may be missing the point. Through the phenomenon of post-charismatics, the movement may come to a clearer understanding of its own specific role within the total context of the Church's life. The spirituality of the movement is Spirit-inspired for evangelization and catechesis, but not necessarily suited for all the other aspects of the Christian life.

Post-charismatics still believe in the movement, but they are in new dimensions of their personal life with God. Occupationally and geographically, their passage through the door of the movement may have left them where they were ten years ago, but they are *not* the same people. They are more mature Christians now. They are able to use the gifts when the Spirit moves, but they no longer *need* to use them. They can still sing in tongues, but generally they may prefer now to let the silent song of their hearts rise to

God. They can profit from the occasional prayer meeting, or attend one out of apostolic concern, but generally they feel they should be loving elsewhere.

As people pass through the movement into other areas of personal/ecclesial life, some of the charismatic elements may be, often are, less visible; they may even cease for a while in this or that person's life. It doesn't necessarily mean that they have lost the gifts or their ability to use them. The Spirit simply may be calling them to a different kind of spirituality, a different kind of mysticism.

Thus, I don't see the renewal as phasing out, not even as reaching a plateau. It is very much alive. We should not see the movement as *dissolving* into larger streams of the Church's life, but as enriching these streams. The movement itself continues to be vitalized by new members and by the strong and faithful dedication of those called by God to foster it. For some people the movement will be a special vocation; for many more, it is proving to be a doorway into the wider streams of the Church's heritage. To repeat: I hope and pray that the movement is not just a phase in the life of the Church. This is the way I hope, one day, all Christians can come to Christ — enthusiastically, and with a wonderful sense of the Lord's love and presence and power! But then, afterwards, the Christian experience of the ages offers other paths and approaches to the Lord.

The ways of the Spirit are manifold. As we enter the eighties and beyond we must have confidence that what the Spirit has done in peoples' lives in the movement is not being washed out but guided. The Spirit is continuing to deepen his life in his people, but often in less charismatic forms of ministry, spiritualities, and life-styles. Wouldn't it imply a lack of faith in the genuineness of the movement if we thought too pessimistically about those who have left and gone elsewhere? Shouldn't we presume that lasting changes have taken place in peoples' hearts? Shouldn't we trust that generally the Spirit is still guiding these people, and that they are still trying to be faithful in following him?

This book, therefore, is meant to be a book of hope. It is based on the conviction that, even though the movement has lost track of hundreds of thousands of people, the wonderful Spirit of Jesus continues to guide them, and they continue to follow.

Two

Enthusiasm in the Spirit: Ten Years After

It is a fact: many thousands of people are no longer involved in the formal renewal. One could object that my positive interpretation of this fact is simply a gratuitous assumption. What criteria can we use to determine if this phenomenon is positive or negative, God's will or not?

Perhaps the only real criterion is hidden in God, for only He knows what is happening in the depths of peoples' hearts. Peoples' own testimony would be valuable, and the fruits of their new way would surely tell us a good deal: "By their fruits you will know them."

But there is also another indicator. One could try to show how or if this post-charismatic spirituality relates to our traditional theological understanding of the growth of the spiritual life. Are the present orientations of post-charismatics unusual, or can we find parallels in the writings of the spiritual masters? This is the subject of the present chapter. It will be a little "heavy going." I ask the reader's indulgence and perseverance and promise the rest of the book will be easier reading! But it is necessary to lay some solid theological groundwork for the post-charismatic spirituality.

In 1975 I wrote a book on the charismatic movement entitled *Enthusiasm In the Spirit*. It dealt with some theological aspects of the renewal with which I had been struggling since my first contact in 1970. Let me say clearly and unambiguously that I still believe whole-heartedly in the work of the Spirit in the renewal. More, I have deepened my conviction that it would be a wonderful blessing if what is happening in the charismatic movement was experienced by all of God's people.

It is becoming more and more obvious that the conscious, experiential awareness of the Spirit, his gifts and fruits, is a factor in our catechesis and understanding of Christian life which has been sadly neglected. I don't know about the reader, but I once believed that grace cannot really be experienced.

Karl Rahner has disassociated himself from the particular theological school which would make the life of grace occur in a totally *unconscious* realm of the human person. He simply asks the question, "Have we ever actually experienced grace?" then answers in the affirmative by describing human experiences of self-sacrificing love. Example: "Have we ever forgiven someone even though we got no thanks for it and our silent forgiveness was taken for granted? Once we experience the spirit in this way, we (at least, we as Christians who live in faith) have also *in fact* experienced the *supernatural*."[1] In more recent writings he expands this teaching and concludes that a definite theological interpretation can be given to intense conversion experiences, the reception of the Spirit, baptism in the Spirit, and other such phenomena.[2]

I continue to believe that the experiential nature of the charismatic movement is one of its most important aspects and a key to where post-charismatics are headed. It seems clear that the Father really wants to give each of his children an experience of his great love for them. It is this experience which makes the transition from Jesus as "Saviour of the World" to Jesus as "my Saviour." Only the living Spirit of Jesus can make this truth a felt reality in the heart.

Karl Rahner points to the function of such religious experiences. He says that it helps people break out of a piety which rests solely on conceptual and propositional reflection. Through such experiences, people come face to face with their own inner reference to God. Many Christians live on religious *concepts,* and do not have a personal relationship with God on any deep level.[3]

Surely one of the main thrusts of the Spirit's work in the charismatic movement has been to open people to an experience of God which then becomes central to their lives, unifying – conceptually and practically – all their other religious knowledge and experience.

What is the situation, then, of ordinary Christians in their daily piety? They have at their disposal a large store of religious concepts, propositions, motivations and patterns of behaviour which all perform an important function in guiding their daily life and action. But in their daily affairs they do not encounter with any clarity either the heart of their own subjectivity or God himself in his true self-communication.[4]

This is basically what the Spirit has taught us in the charismatic movement – the tremendous importance of such an experiential encounter with God. We have discovered that without this, most of our catechesis is backwards. Trying to give "religious instructions" to people who have not experienced God the Father through the Spirit of Jesus is not only enormously difficult, but one wonders if it should be done at all.

On the other hand, we have discovered that once people have really accepted Christ in their hearts, and experienced his personal love for them, then further instruction is a genuine pleasure. People gobble up conferences and tapes and books and (yes) even homilies like thirsty wanderers in the desert.

What a joy it is to address people who are really eager to hear about Christ and the teachings of the Church! Isn't this what "teaching Christian doctrine" is all about – what it really should be! Can we continue to disregard these implications of religious experience for catechesis? Can we continue to operate on a theory of "unconscious grace?"

But all these things have been said before. The question which concerns us here is: Where does the charismatic, experiential spirituality "fit in" in the total journey of the soul towards God?

This is a very tricky and delicate question. After struggling with it in prayer and study for many months, I am convinced that it does not admit of any easy or simplistic answers. But I think it *is* possible to give, certainly not definitive, but some tentative directions in which to pursue further insights. It is a question which needs to be addressed if we are to reflect responsibly on the phenomenon of thousands of people leaving the formal renewal.

Scripture calls us to "Be perfect as your heavenly Father is perfect." In the course of the centuries, various names have been given to this perfection. Clement of Alexandria, in the second century, saw the Christian as the true "gnostic", the one who possessed the true "knowledge" of God. At another juncture, the word "mystic" was given to Christian perfection, especially in the works of Evagrius of Ponticus (4th cent.). In the course of time, that word—mystic—took on special connotations, so that after a while only certain people were described as "mystics," and others were not.

How would we put it today? What would be an unequivocal way of saying what all Christians are called to? I think we would say that we are all called to the perfection of *love*. But for my purposes here, and because of Rahner's position that grace—the self-communication of God—can be experienced, I also wish to use the word "mysticism" as synonymous with love. The word "mystic" usually connotes somebody who has experiences of God. All Christians experience God, but in different ways, in different forms. Hence, I want to use our various experiences of God as a way of locating peoples' relationship to the charismatic movement.

In his very important article,[5] Rahner makes a distinction between "genuine mysticism," and "mysticism in ordinary dress," or "mysticism for the masses." He uses these two latter phrases to designate "experiences of the Spirit, glossolalia, the experience of a radical transformation of the old man' into a new person . . . a radical conversion, and similar events which occur today in the various charismatic movements. . . ."[6] Let us take a brief look at each of these two kinds of mysticism.

God can be consciously experienced, says Rahner, but this can happen in a variety of ways. He uses the word "genuine" for a very rarified kind of experience of God in absolute faith, with the bare minimum of mediation through sense, locutions, etc. He says a "clear dose" of this kind of experience is rare. In an earlier article, Rahner gave the opinion that the majority of Christians "do not end up in mysticism (at least if we take mysticism in the sense in which it was understood by the classical Spanish mystics)."[7] My interpretation is that these great mystical writers are in the area of his notion of "genuine mysticism," and that the majority of Christians are not called to meet God *in this way*.

But all Christians are called to the perfection of love. So there must be, says Rahner, a way of experiencing God, a way of having God's love revealed to us, a way of meeting God face to face, that is available to all. This takes place in the phenomena of religious enthusiasm. It is mysticism, the experience of God, in ordinary dress, a mysticism for the masses.

These terms are in no way meant to be derogatory. They are quite positive and meant to give a theological interpretation to the action of the Spirit. Such experiences really reach God in himself, and touch the religious subject in his or her very center. But because we are dealing here with words, emotions, psychological states, etc. which are the media of such experience, discernment and critical judgment are required. "We are not faced with the alternatives of being forced either to recognize expressions of religious enthusiasm . . . as the unadulterated operation of the Holy Spirit, or to discount them from the start . . . as the result of human religious impulses going off the rails."[8] The main thrust of his article is to validate the possibility of religious experiences as true experiences of grace, of God.

Two clarifications. I don't know what German word Rahner used for "genuine," but he certainly means that the "mysticism for the masses" is also "genuine" in our ordinary English understanding of that word. Secondly, I don't think Rahner means to imply (and I certainly don't) that the phenomena he mentioned—glossolalia and similar gifts which occur today in the various charismatic movements—are the *only* kind of mysticism for the masses. It seems clear that he was addressing himself to the charismatic movement, but that he does not intend to exclude a variety of experiences from "mysticism for the masses."

Still using this category of religious experience as a sort of sliding scale, I wish to speak now of the situation of post-charismatics. In order to do so, let me inject here a personal sharing from my own life.

As part of my own spiritual journey, I was in a Trappist monastery before I was eighteen and in a Carthusian monastery before I was twenty-one.

(I kid people that I am now writing a book on stability!) I can truthfully say that my deepest experiences of the transcendence of God were in those monasteries, in an atmosphere of silence, solitude, prayer, community, and hard manual work. During those years I never sang in tongues, prophesied, healed anyone physically, or even prayed out loud spontaneously. There was no real witnessing in the sense we know it in the renewal (although there was much talk about God). I had never attended a charismatic convention (they hadn't begun then), nor saw anyone rest in the Spirit. When I left the Carthusians I surely was not a charismatic in the renewal sense of that word, nor was I meeting God in a mysticism of the masses.

In 1970 I came into contact with the charismatic movement. I helped to start a prayer group. I learned many things about the gifts and prayer meetings. I cannot say I "came to Christ" in the charismatic movement or had a "conversion." I just experienced a wonderful new dimension of my Christian life. I have never ceased praising and thanking God for all these blessings. It really was—and still is—a marvelous *part* of my spiritual journey, another *way* in which I encounter God.

But even now, after years of varying degrees of formal involvement in the renewal, I can still honestly say that no experiences of God in the renewal were more profound than what I experienced in the monasteries. The former were often more joyful, more exuberant, and had other tonalities which the latter often lacked, but I believe my monastic experiences were the deeper of the two.

Very early into the renewal the desire for this other kind of mysticism (what to call it?), which I had experienced in the monasteries, began to surface. There was a longing within me for these quieter waters, a nostalgia for a way to God that was less filled with words and songs and ideas, and, yes, even less filled with imaginative visions and displays of power. There was a longing for an "en-thusiasm," a "being-in-God" which was more direct, more simple.

Here is where I have to be careful. This was (is) *my* experience. Am I going to say that this is where post-charismatics are headed also? The matter can be put differently: Is *my* experience part of a wider pattern, a larger movement of the Spirit, which is also *ordinary* in the lives of Christians? Is this tendency towards a simpler kind of religious experience (mysticism) part of the Spirit's activity among Christians of every age? Can people reach a stage in their spiritual growth where God calls them to radically de-emphasize experiential mediums of religious enthusiasm and meet him more in the darkness of faith?

My answer would be yes, of course. Between the "genuine" mysticism of the rarified kind, and the mysticism of the masses, might there not be a wide landscape and spectrum of mysticism? Assuredly there is. And I think its articulation is found quite obviously in what is traditionally known as the "three ages of the spiritual life," the "purgative, illuminative, and unitive ways." These stages have their origins in the works of Gregory of Nyssa, were more specifically delineated by Pseudo-Denis (who was the first to use these three terms), and subsequently elaborated upon by many spiritual writers down through the ages. Before briefly looking at Gregory of Nyssa, a few comments about how I hope to use this schema in the present discussion.

Rahner has shown how problematic it is to come up with a schema or paradigm of spiritual growth into which everyone can be inserted. He believes it is possible but that we do not yet have one. Each individual is unique, and God's grace is free.

Having pointed out the problems, however, he makes the following statement:

> There is first of all the fact that in some sense or other, and in some form or other, there must be something like a way to Christian perfection, a way which is formed by or divisible into different stages; for unless this be presupposed, the continual and always renewed attempt to define these stages in greater detail – as found in the whole of Christian religion – becomes absolutely incomprehensible and absurd.[9]

Also, I wish to make it clear that I am not equating involvement in the charismatic movement with any of the three stages. The *individual* could be in any or all of the three stages and also be involved in the charismatic movement. What I wish to point out is that, in the framework of these traditional three ways, there is theological justification for people to move out of a charismatic mysticism into a mysticism described in other stages of the spiritual life. Let us now turn to Gregory and a brief account of these stages.

In the history of spirituality it is commonly accepted today that St. Gregory of Nyssa (4th cent.) is a towering figure. His thought on the spiritual life was so fertile and rich that, in Louis Bouyer's opinion, it inspired three of the strongest currents of spirituality emanating from the early centuries. The teachings of Evagrius, Macarius, and Pseudo-Denis are all dependent upon Gregory, each developing different aspects of his thought.[10]

In one of the most beautiful books I have ever read, Jean Danielou's *Platonisme et Theologie Mystique, Doctrine Spirituelle de Saint Gregoire de Nysse*, we find a synthesis of the Saint's teaching on the spiritual life. The book's three main divisions indicate the three stages of the journey. Part One is called "Light or Purification"; Part Two is "The Cloud or Contemplation"; Part Three is "Darkness or Love."

For Gregory, the figure of Moses as the friend of God forms the biblical framework for his understanding of the spiritual life:

The manifestation of God was first made to Moses in light; then he spoke with him under the cloud; finally, having become perfect, Moses contemplated God in darkness. The passage from darkness to light is the first separation from false and erroneous ideas about God. Then, the intelligence, more attentive to hidden things, leads the soul by visible realities to the invisible reality. This is like a cloud which obscures everything sensible and accustoms the soul to hidden contemplation. Finally, the soul which has moved along by these roads towards things on high . . . penetrates into the sanctuary of divine knowledge surrounded on all sides by the divine darkness.[11]

Danielou writes:

> The beginning of the spiritual life is presented under the double aspect of separation and illumination . . . illumination of the soul by the burning bush which is the Word Incarnate calling us higher. The crossing of the desert under the cloud situates us in the second way: disaffection from earthly things and accustoming ourselves to live a life of faith. Finally, on the top of Mt. Sinai, the entrance into the darkness draws us into the mystical life.[12]

The illumination by the burning bush, the crossing of the desert, and the envelopment by the divine darkness are not, of course, mutually exclusive experiences, but they definitely *do* describe the predominant spiritual atmosphere and path of the soul on its journey towards God. As Rahner said, there must be "something to it" if countless spiritual masters have used this paradigm. It is not simply a theoretical construct into which spiritual experiences are fitted. Rather, *people have been experiencing these stages and have sought to describe them.*

The temptation now would be simply and neatly to say that the charismatic movement is the burning bush experience. It is not that easy. People come into contact with the charismatic movement at all different stages of their spiritual journeys.

For some, the charismatic movement may well have been the burning bush experience, the wonderful experience of God breaking in on their sheep-herding. It may well have been one's first encounter with the living God in the midst of the fire. It may well have been the passing from cold and/or no faith into the transcendent experience of light and purification. It may well have been the difference between Christ and no Christ, between light and darkness.

On the other hand, many already may have met Christ and given him their lives. They may have seen the burning bush half-way across the desert. The charismatic movement was a further manifestation of God's presence and guidance, but not their first real encounter with him.

Still others already may have been ascending the mount of divine darkness and experienced no real attraction to remain in the charismatic movement. (I think this is the reason why monastic communities, who live by a different kind of mysticism, often choose not to incorporate the charismatic movement into their spirituality.)

Therefore, while it is not possible to perfectly equate the charismatic movement with the first stage (burning bush) of a person's journey towards God, it *is* possible to equate it with the mysticism for the masses, which by definition emphasizes religious enthusiasm and therefore illumination. In one very important sense, then, the charismatic movement is a burning bush experience, understood as the conscious awareness of the Spirit and his gifts. It may have occurred at Horeb (Ex. 3), at the beginning of one's spiritual journey; it may have occurred during one's desert journey; it may have occurred closer to one's approach to the divine mountain. The precise *meaning* of this illumination must be determined in the context of each individual life.

I would like to return, now, to the different kinds of mysticism. Without implying that those who remain in a more charismatic kind of mysticism remain standing in front of the burning bush, that is, remain in the first stage of illumination; without trying to *measure love* or who is *progressing better,* I wish to give as my opinion that many post-charismatics are moving away from a mysticism of religious enthusiasm into a kind of mysticism which corresponds more to the second stage of the journey through the desert. And this movement away from more experiential media in our life with God accords very well with what the spiritual masters describe as the characteristics of the journey.

It is not my intention to give the classical descriptions of these characteristics. One can read them in any number of treatises.[13] While some people may be called all their lives to travel within a pronounced charismatic framework, we must see clearly that many people will also be called to a different kind of spirituality.

It will be a spirituality fully conscious of the gifts, and free to use them when the occasions present themselves, but it will not make the use of the gifts the focal point for Christian existence. It will be a spirituality drawn to channel the Spirit's energies into deeper silence, more private prayer, a prayer which emphasizes stillness and repose rather than external expressions. It will be a spirituality where people pray over each other for healing at home, using less formulae and techniques, simply allowing the healing love of Jesus to pass through them.

It will be a spirituality where prophetic words of life are spoken more as integrated parts of conversations, like Jesus speaking with the woman at the well. It will be a spirituality where witnessing occurs more naturally, more effortlessly, waiting for the graced moment at home, work, or play, in order to share with others the wonderful works of God. It will be a spirituality where bible reading, alone or with others, is as common and as essential as eating food.

It will be a spirituality where people, having become more sensitized to their own interior needs, are able to pursue their individual paths with the help of a director or a "prayer partner," someone with whom they meet on a regular basis for mutual prayer and discernment. It will be a spirituality where prayers of exorcism are said frequently for protection, and where the power of love, the sacraments and sacramentals, and constant vigilance safeguard people from the attacks of the evil ones.

It will be a spirituality attuned to the Spirit as he attempts to integrate the charisms, in his own gentle way, into the ordinary structures of parish, family, and neighborhood. It will be a spirituality less dependent upon religious enthusiasm and more desirous of drinking at quieter fountains of grace.

In *Enthusiasm In the Spirit*[14] I wrote about the charismatic movement of Montanism in the second century. Because of aberrations at that time, the Church over-reacted, and this led to the gradual loss in the Church of some of the gifts of the

Spirit such as prophecy. We should all be rejoicing today in the wonderful guidance being given in the charismatic movement on the meaning, use, and place of the gifts in the lives of God's people. The eighties may be the decade of perspective, the decade for seeing the place of the renewal in the total life of the Church and of individuals. But there are other enthusiasms in the Spirit besides the charismatic. The gifts remain, but their use and expression can take on new forms.

What name shall we give this mysticism which lives out the power of the Spirit in quieter, more hidden ways? What should we call the mysticism which somewhat leaves behind the excited feelings of having seen the burning bush? What shall we call the mysticism of the long haul, of the trek across the desert? What shall we call the mysticism of, not simply the ordinary, but the extraordinary ordinary, the ordinary filled with the Spirit's presence? May we not call it the mysticism of Nazareth?

People are looking down the road and asking themselves, "What is the long-range plan, what is the spirituality for the next twenty, thirty, or forty years of my life?" For many the answer will be, "The spirituality of Nazareth." Nazareth is not simply a place where we prepare for a ministry beyond our homes. It may be that for some. But for many others, *Nazareth is their ministry,* their ordinary way of living the life in the Spirit.

One indication of this movement towards Nazareth is the increased devotion to Mary in the charismatic renewal over the past few years. Whoever is attracted to Mary, is attracted to Nazareth, and the kind of spirituality she lived there.

Every once in a while you read pamphlets or articles about Mary as the "Model Charismatic," or the "Ideal Charismatic." But when you read these articles you can't really find anything charismatic about Mary in the sense in which that word is used in the charismatic movement. As far as I understand it, "charismatic renewal" refers precisely to the renewal of the charisms — tongues, prophecy, healing, etc. Calling Mary the "Model Charismatic" is a good example of how "charismatic" or "charismatic renewal" becomes the prime analogue, the umbrella under which everything must come, or to which everything must be referred.

In one very real sense, Our Lady does not come across (from what we know of her in the gospels) as anyone approaching a charismatic person! She may have sung in tongues with the apostles on Pentecost, but beyond that, we never see her healing, casting out demons, preaching, witnessing, or prophesying.

Just as, in one sense, Mary is not the model apostle (she never founded any church), the model preacher (no record of her having done so), the model healer (no instance of it happening), so we can say she is not the model charismatic either.

On the other hand, because she is the perfect Christian, possessing the fullness of the gifts and the fruits of the Spirit, she is the Queen of Apostles, the Queen of Preachers, the Queen of Healers, and the Queen of Charismatics.

What is pointed out about Mary in these articles? A woman of faith. Perfect Temple of the

Spirit. True model of prayer. Lived perfectly the Word of God. But I think it's misleading to call these characteristics of her spiritual life "charismatic."

When we look towards Mary, what we see most of all is the perfection of the *fruits* of the Spirit — love, joy, peace, patience, kindness, goodness, fidelity, gentleness, self-control. Mary is indeed the model of these virtues. Devotion to her is leading post-charismatics into an age of the *fruits* of the Spirit. Mary will be a primary model for the post-charismatic.

The gifts are *for the fruits.* "Prophecies will cease, tongues will be silent, knowledge will pass away" (1 Cor. 13:8). On the list of priorities, there is something *secondary* about the gifts. We have all experienced how the gifts were often given an importance to the detriment of the fruits. Is it not almost a characteristic of early involvement in the charismatic movement to have fights over the gifts? Could it not be that now the fruits are being given their rightful priority, and the gifts are taking second place?

It is not a matter of a rejection of the gifts; post-charismatics still believe in them and use them when the Spirit invites. But people are much more sensitive now to the importance of peace and love and joy *even over the use of the gifts.* People are becoming more sensitive to what can destroy the precious interior fruits of the Spirit. Whereas in the past they may have tended to use their gifts "no matter what," we are now seeing people live more exclusively by the fruits, without a pronounced exercise of the gifts for a variety of reasons.

I see this tendency as indicative of a Nazareth spirituality. Many people who have come into the experience of the burning bush and the annunciation of the good news, have gone immediately into ministry without spending sufficient time in Nazareth. This is especially true of those for whom the charismatic movement was their initial coming to Christ, their first experience of the living God in the fire, their shock of being knocked off their horses on their way to madness.

Post-charismatics are entering some period of deeper life. The eighties may be the decade where we see more clearly the kind of preparation needed before Christians engage in public ministry for the Lord. It may be the decade where we acquire a deeper understanding of the rhythms of withdrawal and activity necessary for sustained involvement. It may be the decade of greater insight as to how the spirituality of the charismatic movement fits into the total journey of the person on the way to the mountain of the divine darkness.

Three

The Return to Nazareth

At this juncture I will put two images together: Nazareth and the desert (Chapter Four). I do not wish to confuse these rich biblical images, but in one way they are very similar: both are long, intense periods during which the ways of God are burned into one's soul.

When Gregory uses the desert as his image for the second stage of the spiritual journey, I see this not so much as Jesus' forty days of preparation but as the longer period of the forty years God's people spent in the wilderness. It seems to me that this second stage – after the enlightenment and before the ascent to the divine darkness – is the longest stage, the "long haul," as I call it.

John the Baptist spent most of his adult life in the desert, and Jesus called him the greatest born of woman. Mary was illumined at the Annunciation, filled with the Spirit, then spent long years nurturing the Word in her womb and in her home. Paul, after his burning bush experience on the road to Damascus, went off to Arabia, presumably for a period of prayer and reflection about his future mission. Then there is the prime example of Jesus spending thirty years in Nazareth, which is the subject of this chapter.

Ideally (which means it hardly ever happens!), we should not venture forth for ministry until we can at least see the outline of the mountain of God as we emerge from the desert. At that stage, our hearts would be fairly purified, we would have experienced God's love, care, and protection, and we would have seen something of the vision to which we would then try to give witness. We would know something of the cost of following the Lord, our spiritual muscles would have been tested by the heat of the desert—in short, we would be ready for the onslaught of Jericho.

But living in the actual world as we all do, we frequently are preaching eloquently from hearsay about the vision of God, since we ourselves are struggling in the desert and have not actually seen the mountain. Not having traveled very far into the desert, we are naive about our capacities to take over the citadels of the pagan territories. In one sense, Nazareth can be understood as this period of preparation that would be desirable for all. Jesus lived in Nazareth a *long time.*

Whenever we think of "imitating Jesus" or following him, our thoughts more often than not turn to his public life. This is understandable. This is what the gospels are all about; this is what we know most about him. It is also powerful and glorious and challenging. So, we meditate on his preaching to the multitudes, and even envision this as a goal for ourselves. We watch him heal and cast out demons. "Greater works than these shall you do," he has said to us, and our hearts thrill at the prospect.

What we fail to take equally as seriously, though, is Jesus' life in Nazareth *before* his public ministry. His public ministry lasted only a very short time, perhaps not even three years. Not long, really, considering he was God, the Saviour of the world, and would only live one life like our own. People in the charismatic movement are attracted especially to the public life, since it deals with the use of the charisms such as healing, deliverance, and preaching with power. But, has *Nazareth* preceded our ministry of power?

In one real sense, we have all left Nazareth too soon. We have left prematurely, before it was "our time," before we knew what the gospel really was, before we really knew how to love, how to pray. Impelled by a variety of needs within and without, we have thought that the preaching of the gospel was the really hard task. No. The harder challenge is living completely in Nazareth. The ministry is hard primarily because we have not prepared well enough in Nazareth.

What do I mean by Nazareth? Well, for Jesus, it actually was a very long period of time. We reckon thirty years. We like to take the gospel texts about his preaching and healing *literally* (and we should), but do we take *Nazareth literally?* Yes, we want to imitate Jesus, but, really, the *waste* of Nazareth! There is so much to be done. Yes, we have our preparations for ministry—study programs, retreats, seminars, conventions, novitiates, houses of formation, seminaries. But usually the time spent there is short, and quite inadequate. There is an anxiety, an impatience to "get started" because the "needs are so great."

The needs were great in Jesus' day also; they are always enormous. To paraphrase the gospel we might say, "Overwhelming needs you always have with you." But even in the face of such needs Jesus spent thirty years in silence and obscurity. He simply lived like anybody else. He learned how to be human. He worked with his hands. He loved the people with whom he lived and, generally, *did,* on a day to day basis, all the things he would one day *preach* to the multitudes.

Either one of two things: 1) He really *was* wasting his time there, or 2) by living so long in Nazareth he was trying to communicate to us some profound truths about human life, about how to become his disciples in the service of the gospel. Our faith must choose the latter explanation!

Many of the great missionaries and bishops in the early centuries of the Church were monks who were called out of their monasteries. This seems ideal to me, although the long period of preparation may not require a monastic setting. In a relatively short time, these men accomplished incredible feats of missionary and apostolic activity. How? Because they had spent years in prayer, hard work, community life, and study. They were finely honed instruments. They had crossed much of the desert. They had seen the mountain. Now they were ready to spend the rest of their lives in a powerful and undivided shepherding of God's people. They often accomplished extraordinary apostolic endeavors in a relatively short period of time because they were *ready.*

To all this it may be countered that when the Lord sent out the seventy-two disciples, there was no prolonged Nazareth preparation. Let me make some observations.

First, it is very different to be directly discipled by the Lord Jesus himself! Secondly, they were sent out "before him," that is, as a preparation for his own coming into those towns. Thus, they were not responsible for the whole mission but were heralds of the coming of the Master.

Thirdly, Jesus was very selective in the people he chose. The rich young man, who had lived a long and good life, was considered ready by the Lord, and was invited – but the young man refused. Another man who had just been cured asked to become an immediate disciple, but Jesus did not think he was ready, and sent him back home.

People come into contact with the charismatic movement having a variety of backgrounds. Some, like the rich young man, have been living a godly life for many, many years. They, perhaps, are more ready for a ministry with the gifts of power. Others (like the man who was cured) literally come from darkness to light. They have no solid faith background. Jesus sent such people back home for a while. But often, such people are propelled prematurely into ministry.

Others may be in an in-between stage. They are able to sustain a ministry for a few years, then realize their weak foundations and their need for more spiritual maturity.

Because our preparations are poor, we spend a great deal of time commuting between Nazareth and Jerusalem. This commuting is not simply getting away for times of prayer and refreshment; Jesus also did this during his public life. No. It is something far different, far more basic. Because our preparation was defective, we arrive at periods in our lives where we sense that we cannot really continue on in any meaningful way unless we retreat and build deeper foundations. We realize we have left Nazareth too soon.

This is not out of the ordinary, of course. How many people have had the opportunity, the wisdom, the courage, the time to spend half a lifetime in preparation for ministry! It's an inconceivable proposal for us. To take it seriously would revolutionize our whole approach to the apostolate. Yet, Jesus did it. I think if we could ever arrive at this kind of wisdom and restraint, our ministries would possess an unbelievable and wonderful fruitfulness.

The charismatic movement has been clarifying many aspects of the Christian life. Could this be a further clarification? We are in such a great hurry to get out and serve the needs of humankind. People who have met the Lord Jesus Christ in a new and powerful way and then spent a few years learning and exercising the gifts of spiritual power – are they really *ready* to attack Jericho! In Jacques Ellul's *False Presence of the Kingdom,* he writes:

What I am saying is that we are sending into the world babes in arms, who are not yet ready for adult tasks, that there is a preparaion, both spiritual and intellectual, ethical and sociological, meditative and active, which is in *no way* being given to the Church, nor to those in the Church whom we are urging to become involved in the world.[1]

I wish to call attention to the fact that the demands of Nazareth are very great, and that's one of the reasons we can't wait to leave and "get going."

It seems paradoxical to say this, especially since many programs are being offered in the charismatic movement, but I think many post-charismatics are returning to Nazareth to learn there what they missed the first time around. It is not simply in the area of instruction. Their hearts are still longing to preach the gospel and to use their gifts for the Lord. But they sense that something deeper must happen to them before they embark on any more ministry. They are seeking some "depth-quality" to their being. The remainder of this book concerns certain areas of Christian life which post-charismatics are being called to deepen at this time, and they are being called to deepen them precisely in Nazareth.

Some of these post-charismatics are being called to Nazareth *because of their circumstances.* They would *like* to remain involved in renewal programs, would *like* to have more real community support, but may not find it possible. God speaks to us through our circumstances and responsibilities.

I think these people need to be given *hope* that God will not abandon them, that the Spirit will guide them and feed them in his own mysterious ways. But to see his action where they are, they have to *be* where they are, accept where they are, and not feel guilty for being where they are. This instinct of *being* is expressed by a phrase current among post-charismatics: "Bloom Where You Are Planted." Precisely! If we can't bloom where we are, we misunderstand the mystery of Nazareth.

During his public ministry, Jesus could spend nights in prayer and days in the marketplace because, before he left Nazareth, he was in perfect harmony in his own personal solitude before the Father. Nazareth is the place where we learn how always to *be* before the Father's face. Then we never leave his presence. We are no longer afraid of God, no longer using activity as an escape from our interior solitude and loneliness. In Nazareth, one learns how to close the gap between "activity" and "contemplation." In Nazareth, action eventually becomes one of many expressions of love and adoration of the Father. A wholeness is achieved there. "I am not alone, the Father is always with me," said the Lord. Even in the midst of the crowds, Jesus was always in communion with the Father.

I think many people in the renewal began to realize that they did not have the interior strength with which to meet the demands of ministry. They were simply exhausted, burnt out. This could have resulted from a lack of *discernment* as to their abilities. I want to describe here what often is the dynamics of this spiritual exhaustion. It could happen in regard to any of the gifts, but I will use deliverance as my example.

We have become very aware in the charismatic movement that we are dealing with real spiritual power. This power is a two-edged sword: it is capable of being used properly as well as abused.

It has become evident that people's ministry and use of this spiritual power can move beyond their own personal growth and maturity; that is, a person can find himself "over his head." This can be due to imprudence, pride, or any number of other factors. Let me use deliverance as an example, because, potentially, it is capable of causing the most damage, both to the unity of Christians and to the deliverer and deliveree.

Jesus quite plainly wishes to give this power to his disciples. "Jesus summoned the Twelve and began to send them out in pairs giving them authority over the unclean spirits" (Mk 6:7). It is clear from other passages (i.e., the ending of Mark's gospel) that the early Church understood it had this power from the Lord.

But there is another strain of thought which was part of the early Church's thinking, and it is stated in Matthew 7:21-23: "Not everyone who says 'Lord, Lord,' will enter the kingdom of God, but only the one who does the will of my Father in heaven. When that day comes, many will plead with me, 'Lord, Lord, have we not prophesied in your name? Have we not exorcised demons by its power? Did we not do many miracles in your name as well?' Then I will declare to them solemnly, 'I never knew you. Out of my sight, you evildoers!'"

Often this passage is used by people who do not understand the place of the gifts in the life of the Church. We cannot deny, however, that there is a remarkable and enormously important distinction made here, *a distinction between the use of spiritual power in the Lord's name and doing the will of the Father.* They are not necessarily the same thing! This is really an astounding truth. If it were not so clearly stated in the gospel, we would certainly hesitate to make it. Quite simply it means this: If you prophesy, or cast out demons, or heal people in Jesus' name, it doesn't guarantee that *by that act* you are doing what is pleasing to the Father.

There is a deep mystery here. Paul says that God does not take back his gifts. He has given us Jesus, and Jesus is Lord, and his Name has power. It is his *Name* that has the power. We can easily reason that if I am using Jesus' name, and all sorts of wonderful things are happening, then it is God's will.

Spiritual power is fascinating and intoxicating – understandably so. Thus a great deal of spiritual maturity is required to exercise it. Here is where a profound discernment is required. In early stages of involvement in the charismatic movement, people learn about the gifts and how to use them. This discovery is wonderful and exhilarating, because it deals with spiritual power. However, the second stage of the Spirit's instruction about the gifts concerns a more disciplined use of spiritual power. He instructs us to be more sensitive as to when, how, and even *if* to use such power. Simply throwing spiritual power around is not the same as doing God's will.

Post-charismatics are asking themselves more earnestly some of the following questions: "What is my motivation? Am I out for personal glory? Am I on an ego trip? Am I being imprudent? Do I have enough experience? Are my gifts under submission to anyone? Do I belong to a community of any kind, so that there is a context for discernment in the use of my gifts? Am I simply being pulled around by peoples' needs? Do I equate peoples' needs with the will of God, and is it his will that *I* help them? Am I aware of the danger of exercising spiritual power? Am I seeking notoriety? Am I really a person of prayer? Do I lead a disciplined life? Am I willing to submit the exercise of my gifts in obedience to someone else's discernment? Would I stop using them if this person told me to do so? Do I have a spiritual head of any kind? A spiritual director? Is the maturity of my Christian life keeping pace wi h my ministry, with the number of people coming to me?"

People exercising the gifts in Jesus' name can become bruised and battered by the abuse of spiritual power. Merely the fact that Jesus' name "works" is not enough. Are *we* working? Is our Christian life keeping pace with our ministry and use of the gifts? If we can ever put these two things together – the power of the name of Jesus, *and* deep love, prudence, submission, and humility, then we will begin to see something of the gentle, disciplined strength of real spiritual power which we see in Christ.

Another reason for withdrawal from the formal renewal is the greater *discernment* people are exercising, not only as regards the use or abuse of the gifts, but in regard to the use of their *time* as well. Greater discernment about the *priorities* in their lives actually has led many people to use their time elsewhere. This may well be another characteristic of the post-charismatic phenomenon.

Many people have decided that they have just so much time and energy. After sincere prayer and heart-searching, they have decided that God really wants them elsewhere than in the formal renewal. They are achieving greater clarity as to which inspirations really are God's will for them and which are simply good in themselves.

Stage #1 of discernment is separating the good from the evil. Stage #2 is separating the good from the good — good in general from good for *me*, God's special will for me. The enthusiasm of the charismatic movement tends to make people run in ten directions at once. All the needs seem legitimate, and, after all, isn't that what the gifts are for? We are bombarded by so many good intentions and inspirations, that we literally do not know how we can respond to them all!

"Good" inspirations can come from our pride, as when we are attempting things beyond our powers. "Good" inspirations can be alien to the actual vocation to which God has called us. "Good" inspirations can come from evil spirits.

I think it needs to be said clearly that many post-charismatics have achieved a greater clarity and discernment as to how they are to use their time and talents. They should not be made to feel guilty for leaving the formal renewal, for that *really may be part of God's plan for them in their actual situation.*

I think many people realized that if they were to continue on in the life of the Spirit, they had to learn, among other things, how to pray better — not prayer in a group, but the prayer of silence and solitude, a kind of prayer where they enter dimensions of their interiority not possible in a group.

At the present time there is a movement back to the desert. It is not an escape. It is one of the Christian responses to the challenges of the times which demand greater interior resources and grounding in faith. We have always believed that our own personal life with God is "the soul of the apostolate." For a while, prayer meetings and the spirituality of the charismatic movement were sufficient, but then, for many, it ceased to be deep enough. The fruitfulness of our ministry will always depend on how deeply we can *be* before the Father. Many people are returning to Nazareth to learn how to do this better.

Chapter Four deals with the deepening of the journey inward which is often accompanied by a change in prayer forms and by different ways of expressing our love for God.

One of the factors, I think, which can inhibit growth in the Spirit in the charismatic movement, is the stereotyped expressions of prayer and prayer meetings. Our God is a God who creates new things; he is the Creator. Personal relationships demand newness. We do not (or ought not!) keep saying the same stereotyped things to people we love. Nor does the person in love with God. Our dialogue with God should constantly grow and change, and the Spirit is at work seeking to put new words of love on our lips.

Many people feel "locked in" to charismatic expressions and prayer patterns which no longer express for them their continuing, developing relationship with God. At a certain point they leave prayer meetings so that their dialogue with God may acquire more and more its own unique expression.

To create a whole new style of prayer meeting to meet this need would require a homogeneity in groups which they often lack. There are always newcomers and "veterans" together. Group leaders seem to have opted (and the Spirit may well be guiding this) for keeping old patterns precisely because of the newcomers. But then, people who have been in the charismatic movement for five or six years no longer find these set patterns meaningful.

Perhaps this is one reason why statistics show almost half of those present at prayer meetings are newcomers. Unless there is some transformation of the old patterns, or unless some other arrangements are made, (perhaps a separate prayer meeting for veterans?), people leave to seek out their own unique prayer expressions. Alone or with a few others, they are exploring new ways of praying and using the gifts.

I believe that many of the people who no longer attend prayer meetings are praying more at home, and that they are praying more in smaller groups of "two and three." When Jesus used this number, "where two or three are gathered in my name," he may have foreseen that this mini-prayer meeting would be closer to the possible daily diet of many of his followers. Maybe people had to be taught through the charismatic movement how to pray together. Now they are returning to Nazareth to pray in smaller groups.

I have no statistics, of course, but I hear of many, many people praying in small groups of twos and threes, in homes, in offices before work, in times of special need. People have learned how to pray together, and they no longer need the larger prayer meeting to the same extent they did before.

Father Basil Pennington has some remarks concerning the relationship between the more quiet kind of centering prayer to which I believe many post-charismatics are being called, and the style of charismatic prayer found in prayer groups. He writes:

> Charismatic prayer, as it has manifested itself and developed in the mainline churches, has tended to take on almost exclusively extroverted forms. When one is first drawn into charismatic prayer, it is usually a very affective prayer, full of very strong feelings and emotions and inviting active expression. But not infrequently it happens that, after a time, one feels drawn to more and more quiet and silence.[2]

Father Basil remarks that this happens to groups as well as to individuals. It is not a question of seeing any opposition between these two forms of prayer, but of seeing them as complementary and of trying to provide ways of expression for quiet prayer. The following paragraph brings out well the movement of grace I am trying to describe throughout this book:

> Some leaders of charismatic prayer meetings have shared with me a certain personal concern. In their ministry they have seen members of their groups ... being drawn into the ways of contemplative prayer, while they themselves are still drawn to praise the Lord very actively in tongues and song.

They wonder if they are missing something, if others are not passing them by. Of course, it is possible that others are passing them by. God is the master of his gifts, and he need not give the most or the best to the leaders. But also . . . one's growth in love – and that is the essential growth in Christian life – is not to be correlated with the kind of prayer one practices. The important thing is to move with the Spirit and to pray as one can. But there may be something else here that an attentive discernment may bring out.[3]

That "something else" is the topic of this book: people can be moved by the Spirit into non-charismatic ways of prayer and devotion. Really, there is only one kind of prayer, the prayer from the heart. Whoever prays from the heart really prays, no matter if it be of the charismatic or more contemplative variety. But for many people, in order for prayer to keep "coming from the heart," a certain progression to more quiet prayer may be necessary. Too many set forms – or too many external forms – may have a retarding effect.

Catherine Doherty speaks of Nazareth as the most perfect family of love that ever existed on this earth. In her book, *The People of the Towel and the Water*,[4] she spells out her vision of how to live the ordinary in an extraordinary way.

Through the charismatic movement, many people received a new vision of this community of love which Jesus meant to be *the sign* of God's presence in the world. Many people left their Nazareths – neighborhoods, parishes, natural relationships – to form a community elsewhere. They gradually realized two things: one, it is not easy to form such a community; and two, that the real challenge for many of them was back in the Nazareths they had left.

Chapter Five, then, deals with the cost of forming a community of love, whether at home or elsewhere, but especially at home, where people are, in Nazareth. I think that only now, after having experienced the renewal, are many people able to return to their Nazareths and pay the high price of unity.

For a while, many were content to commute to prayer meetings and prayer groups. But can this be the long-range plan for their lives? I think many are seeing that the real challenge for them is in their homes and neighborhoods. Projects for more specialized community arrangements have not materialized. There is no hope in the immediate future that too many charismatics will be able to live in such specialized communities. People are returning to their Nazareths, and there are learning how to save the world from their carpenter shops, offices and kitchens – like Jesus and Mary.

It is important to emphasize Nazareth, because in some ways the charismatic movement calls people out of the ordinary. One often hears the call to live in a specialized community. This is one way, and some people will be called to live in such communities; I live in one myself.

But Christianity has never been a cluster of communities living like islands in the midst of the world. One reason for this is that Christians have a tendency to fall in love with people who are not Christians! What if the people you love do not share your dedication and commitment?

Your call, of course, is to stay with them. Post-charismatics are returning to their Nazareths to love the people to whom their lives are bound. A call for everyone to live in specialized communities is unreal, not possible. To over-emphasize it as being the *only way* can frustrate many people.

Chapter Six is a meditation on the cost of winning the world for Christ. When Jesus left Nazareth he knew that sooner or later there would be a head-on collision between his gospel and the powers of evil. He realized clearly that when this confrontation came, he could not and would not resort to any tactics other than love and suffering. There would be no counter-revolution, no violence, no despair—just suffering and love.

We are not too clear about this, nor are we as willing and as able to suffer and love. We did not think, in the early stages of enthusiasm, that it would be so hard to win the world for Christ. We thought, like Peter, we were prepared to go all the way—"Let us go and die with him." But then, when the crunch came, we had second thoughts. We didn't think it would cost our lives. The return to Nazareth is a return to realistically appraising our strengths and weaknesses. It is a time to reconsider the cost of winning the world for Christ.

I think another reason for the return to Nazareth is a deeper appreciation for the nature of the Church (Chapter Seven). The charismatic movement has given people a deeper understanding of the Church, has increased their desire to drink more deeply at the traditional fountains of Church tradition, history, and spirituality. Many no longer find ecclesial depth in the prayer group structures, and are seeking out places where they can enter more deeply into the Church's life.

The Lord's life in Nazareth, in one sense, was very uncharismatic. I do not mean this in any facetious way. But the carpenter's son did not seem memorable to most people. One of the mysteries of Nazareth with which many people must now come to grips is precisely that the outward expression of the gifts is not the only way of living the Christ-life; at least, it may not be the pattern *for every phase* of the Christian journey.

When people return to Nazareth from the charismatic movement, they discover that often circumstances do not allow them to express their gifts. They may live with people who are not even Christians, or with Christians who are being called to God by other paths, or with Christians who do not understand or believe in the gifts. In such situations, they will be led by the Spirit to use their gifts in ways that are more subtle, more hidden.

For many, many reasons the only faith stance possible may be deeply *being* before the Father's face (like Jesus in Nazareth). As I tried to show, our understanding of mysticism allows for many other expressions of love. It is possible to live a profound life in the Spirit without too much external activity of the charismatic kind.

I think Jesus lived so long in Nazareth – and so hiddenly – because that's how most people on earth must spend their existence. They are not preparing for some great mission: *their daily life is their great mission.* If it is not possible to come to the Father in Nazareth, then most people are not going to make it. If it is not possible to come to God simply by loving and by doing what God asks each day, then most people are in an impossible situation. Thus, I do not only see Nazareth as a time of preparation: it is a way of life to which the majority of Christians are called.

I believe Jesus lived in that little, obscure village to say clearly to all of us: "You can come to my Father right where you are. Love one another. Keep the commandments I have given you. Pray. Do this and you shall live."

Increasingly, the literature on mysticism is pointing to the *ordinary* as the atmosphere of final wholeness and synthesis. William Johnston writes:

> Mystical experience may at first be delightful and filled with froth and joy; but eventually the call comes to go deeper and (wonder of wonders) this going deeper in all the great mystical traditions is a *passage to the ordinary* . . . an almost boring silence of penetration and familiarity, a 'becoming at home'. . . . And I wonder if it does not take *another enlightenment of the Spirit to recognize this seemingly hum-drum experience as a real God experience.* (Emphasis added)[5]

This is a confirmation, I believe, of Rahner's distinction between mysticism in ordinary dress, and the mysticism which reaches out to God in the darkness of faith, using less mediums of experience. Is it possible that post-charismatics are sharing in this *second enlightenment* of the Spirit? I think they are.

Yes, there is a danger of labeling as an "enlightenment" what may well be, on the part of some, back-sliding. But I think that many people are now being propelled by the Spirit away from a mysticism of experience into a mysticism of the ordinary. They may not be able to articulate it, but their hearts tell them that they are being called into deeper life.

> But one thing is clear; namely, that the higher stages of the mystical life are very ordinary. There is no ecstasy, no rapture, no flash of light, no bells, no incense. It is a very quiet and simple realization that God is my Father and I, another Christ, am truly his son or his daughter and that the Holy Spirit dwells in me.[6]

Is not this a perfect description of Nazareth?

Lest people returning to Nazareth get discouraged, it must be stated very emphatically, as part of the truth of the Christian message, that God is very powerful, very generous, and very aware of the situation of his children living in the midst of the world. He can and does and will give them his grace and strength. "I do not pray that you take them out of the world, but that you keep them from evil."

The "world" here must mean a geographical place, otherwise Jesus would not allow us to remain in "it" in any way whatsoever. Nor does he counsel that we separate ourselves from it, although the Spirit may lead some people to do so. In religious life, especially, the Church has blessed such a separation assumed out of love for Christ and for the world. But such an existence has always been the *exception*.

By over-emphasizing the "dangers of the world," we can really make Christians doubt the power of God to help them where they are. This would be tragic! Christians have always lived "in the world." "Have courage, I have overcome the world." We should not so emphasize the glories of community life as to undermine people's confidence in God's power at work in the world.

The main lesson of one series of stories from the desert fathers is that there are people in the world living lives of heroic sanctity. Every once in a while the Great Macarius, or St. Anthony, would be called out of his solitude to enter a city and would meet somebody who was really holy! It was God's way of reminding these spiritual giants that He is capable of pouring out oceans of grace on whomever he chooses, no matter where they are. Are these exceptions, or are there countless people of God struggling in the world in a hidden way, and receiving graces beyond our understanding?

I think the latter. Dom Vernor Moore once wrote a book called *The Life of Man With God.* It was based on the results of a survey he took of "ordinary people" living in the world. The survey revealed how extraordinarily holy their lives were, often filled with mystical graces of all kinds.

As we attempt to assess the phenomenon of people passing through the charismatic movement, we need to have a greater trust in God's grace and power; we also need a greater caution in trying to measure grace in terms of externals. We need to humble ourselves before the mystery of grace. "As the heavens are exalted above the earth, so are my ways above your ways, and my thoughts above your thoughts." No one ever has a totally clear grasp on the workings of grace.

The Spirit, it seems to me, is always engaged in leading certain people into new pathways so that they will be able to guide others in the future. Many people are being drawn back to Nazareth in order to acquire wisdom about these further stages in the life of the Spirit.

I do not wish to imply that the spirituality of Nazareth now becomes the prime analogue to which everything must be referred. No. The Lord is supreme in his grace. But as I reflect on the data of revelation, as we acquire a better sense of the spiritual maturity required for Christian ministry, and as we look at the development of the life of grace within us, it seems we need to take more seriously Jesus' life in Nazareth and to explore the meaning of this hidden period for the total life of the Christian.

Jesus, possessing the fullness of the gifts, lived quietly in Nazareth for thirty years. Living deeply before the Father's face, in love, is the heart of the matter. Eventually he was called out, but it was in Nazareth—before the Father—that he always dwelt. Many are returning to Nazareth either to prepare better for future ministry, or to live their simple existence in a new and more extraordinary way.

Finally, there is Mary. When we look at her in Nazareth, what do we see? We see perfect stillness. We see silence. We see her always in the background. We know what she is doing there. She is the perfect listener of the Word, so perfect that the Word leapt down into her womb. She possessed the fullness of the gifts; yet, the gifts are not so much expressed as they are deep reservoirs of quiet but fathomless powers which effect God's work.

Mary is the quintessence of the ordinary. She seldom left Nazareth. We spend many years racing around (actually or interiorly), trying to find God. Mary always knew where God was. Right where she was! She never left the Father's presence.

Mary is our model for the use of the gifts in an ordinary way. Can we doubt that her mere presence was a terror to the demons, a source of healing, her words sparks of fire that went to the heart of her listeners? All this happened naturally, as it were. She knew it was God's work and that she didn't have to work it up somehow. She is the woman of immense silence and ordinariness, but also of incredible spiritual power. Increased devotion to her (which is now taking place) will continue to lead post-charismatics into a deeper and quieter kind of mysticism.

Four

Heading Across the Desert

I think part of the "second enlightenment" is a deeper penetration into the desert. What do I mean by the desert? It actually may mean a physical desert of varying degrees. For at least fifteen years of my life, on and off, I've lived in some kind of physical desert, more or less separated from others. It is definitely a kind of Nazareth situation. This is one form of the desert.

It also is possible to be in physical solitude (as many people are – elderly, sick, psychologically handicapped) without really being in the desert as I understand it. But I know beyond a shadow of a doubt that many other solitary people live in the desert in a deeper sense, perhaps, than any hermit, Trappistine, or Carthusian.

Physical solitude has certain advantages. It often fosters greater awareness of the interior journey and enables one to articulate it better. But the physical desert-dwellers are not necessarily the ones who travel most deeply into the desert, show the greatest generosity, or sacrifice the most to find the Lord of the desert.

There are many people (post-charismatics among them) who may be in the desert but who do not have the time to think or write about it! Because of preoccupations and the demands of love, they may not even have reflective awareness of their journey. Those who live in the physical desert and who write about it may receive much notoriety, but some of the greatest desert-dwellers and adventurers may live in the towns and cities and homes of the world – in Nazareths known only to God.

What do I mean, then, by the desert? The desert is the long journey each person must take alone to God. There is a vast inner landscape of the soul which many people have not even begun to cross. We may be married, we may live in a wonderful religious community, we may be single but surrounded by many real friends. At one basic level, all this does not matter. There is a journey that each of us must take alone. The masters of the spiritual life have mapped it out for us, but, as every seasoned traveler knows, the map is not the same as the terrain! There are expanses of the soul where no one but God can be with us. God has built into us a radical aloneness that only he can fill. It is this journey that I call the desert, and it requires courage to enter these spaces of our interiority where there is no other living being except God.

Oh yes, in faith we know that we are always surrounded by a great cloud of witnesses, the angels and saints. We are all in the Body of Christ, the New Adam, and thus never really alone. But there are recesses of the human spirit where even these relationships fade off into the distance. Perhaps it's something like being alone on a spaceship heading for Mars. I may know in my mind, and see on my instrument panel, that the whole earth is rooting for me and knows where I am.

Yet, out here in the immensity of the universe, I really am alone – except for God.

Post-charismatics are being called into this interior desert in a deeper way. It is drawing many of them into a different spirituality. It is quieter, less visible, less active, more of a waiting upon God to complete his work in them. Some may actually be called to enter a physical desert of some kind – monastery, convent, prayer house. Others may be making their homes more of a house of prayer where people can come for prayer, encouragement and counsel. Some are being called to prolonged intercessory prayer as the form of their desert. For most, it simply may be a deeper journey into the desert, without any new external form whatsoever. But, whatever expression it takes, these new life-styles symbolize deeper exploration into the interior landscape.

For every phase of our interior journey we need models and guides. Consciously or unconsciously, we tend to pattern our religious behaviour on these models, past or present, until such time when we are in touch with our own unique spirituality.

Who will be our desert models? In the formal renewal, the leaders who appear on stages at conventions and the leaders and members of core groups probably function as models. But who will be the models for post-charismatics? It is here that people increasingly will have to turn to our spiritual traditions and to the other spiritualities of the Church. Our Church is so rich! We have saints in all walks of life who have achieved full union with God and who have left us their teachings and the examples of their lives. We should study their lives and read their works. In the contemporary Church also, the Spirit will provide us with the wisdom and models we need for every phase of our journey.

While each of us must travel the interior desert alone, we can share with one another our experiences. What follows contains something of what the Lord has taught me about the desert. I offer it as encouragement from a fellow traveler. Eventually, the Spirit calls each person into deeper interiority. This is another aspect of the return to Nazareth. Deserts are passageways to richer country. For most of us, this new country is not yet in sight. Now is our desert time.

As I began writing this I went before the Lord in prayer and asked him, "Lord, what do *you* wish me to say about the desert?" Almost immediately the word came: "Tell them that *I* am in the desert." This is not a very complicated word, a very sophisticated word; certainly it will not be a new idea to anyone. Yet it needs to be said: God himself is the only reason for wanting to enter more deeply into the desert; the desire to see his face is the only motive powerful enough to keep us journeying; belief in his power is the only support which can prevent us from falling to pieces; and only the actual experience of his presence gives meaning to our desert spaces.

One of the most recurring phrases in the Bible is the Lord reassuring people, "I will be with you." Over and over again the Lord says that there is no place we can go where he will be absent. The real challenge of life is to believe this about our interior journey, our life's mission par excellence. We stop at superficial levels of our being, because we don't really believe that God is present in the desert spaces.

> They cannot scare me with their empty spaces
> Between stars – on stars where no human race is.
> I have it in me so much nearer home
> To scare myself with my own desert places.

Robert Frost

All real salvation happens in the desert. In biblical terms, Moses came out of the desert to his people in Egypt. God purified his people in the wilderness, then used them to bring his revelation to all the peoples of the earth. The great prophets, and especially John the Baptist, came from the furnace of the desert with the messages of fire. Jesus himself issued forth from the silent wombs of the Father, Nazareth, and the physical desert. The messages of salvation of all the other recognized religious geniuses came from the deserts of their own interior journeys.

The same is true of cultural and political "salvations." Great music, art, and poetry were all given birth in personal solitude. They were and are the fruits of long journeys into the interiors of great hearts. Likewise with philosophies and political visions. These may not all be good (for there are many gods in the desert), but it is certain that nothing of breadth and depth and power – nothing of real lasting value for mankind – can come without a desert experience. Salvations from superficial levels of our being are the fads and passing movements of every age. They pass quickly, because the journeys that brought them to us didn't cost anything. No, any real salvation must come from the desert.

Thus, if there is going to be a new wave of spiritual power as a result of the Spirit's action in the charismatic movement, it is certain that it can only come from the desert, from a deeper penetration, on the part of each person, into the depths of the heart's interiority where God dwells. It's because I see this happening in the lives of post-charismatics that I am optimistic. The Spirit *is* leading people into the desert, and there he is preparing some new wells of spiritual power.

Scripture (Lk. 4:1) says that the Spirit *drove* Jesus into the wilderness. The Spirit attempts to drive everyone into the desert, but not everyone goes, or they do not enter very far, or they enter reluctantly, or after a short distance they run back out.

The call to the desert is the call to deeper life. The very dynamism of our spiritual natures pulls us into the depths. Many people spend most of their lives resisting this attraction. Some people, in spite of themselves, are driven into the desert by circumstances. It may be a prison sentence, a serious illness, a "hitting bottom" after years of drugs or sex or the drive for power. These enforced deserts are not necessarily life-giving, but many people, by accepting them, have met the Lord there.

Some people are driven into the desert by the spirit of truth, or poetry, or art, or the desire for world change. Some are driven there more explicitly by the love of God. Some are driven into the desert places by the love of self, or others, in either a healthy or distorted sense of those words. No doubt, the journey into the desert, at least in its early stages, is a combination of many of these values. Basically, it is the search for meaning, a search for the answer to our radical aloneness.

I am sure that my own early movement towards the desert was a combination of many factors. I hope that love for God was prominent among those factors. Another was the desire to help others.

I remember as a young person being on a car trip with my family. At night, we passed over a bridge and, looking down, I could see thousands of lights in the city below. Each light represented for me a person, and I conceived a profound desire to help each of those persons know the meaning of life and to assist them towards God and happiness. But how? From that time on my solution began to center around "getting in touch with God who was actually in touch with each of these millions of people." Through this contact, I would then be in contact with everyone else. This was and still is one of my motives for being in solitude.

Particularly during the last few years in the charismatic movement, the Spirit has been instructing people in the value and power of intercessory prayer. It is this instinct of "being in touch with the One who is in touch with all." In our Catholic tradition, we understand very well people who dedicate their whole lives to prayer on behalf of others. I belive the mystery of intercessory prayer is driving many post-charismatics deeper into the desert.

There was another motive for my own entrance into the desert, which I hardly articulated at the time. But now that I reflect on it, it was more consciously experienced than the others. It was a sharp, almost physical pain of loneliness. It must have been more pronounced than what many people experience, because I find it difficult to imagine how people can live without striving to "get to the bottom" of this ache of the heart. I was determined at an early age to assuage this hunger.

I simply reasoned that there must be a cure for it; there must be a way to satisfy this pain of loneliness. It was in the Carthusians that God drove me into a region of my interior desert where I discovered his abiding presence. From that time on, some twenty years ago now, I have never again been lonely in the sense I was before. I discovered that *God* is in the desert.

There are a variety of experiences in the desert. There is fear, but fear is not the overwhelming, constant experience of the desert. Fear occurs mostly at the beginning of a new turn on the path, at the top of a new rise on the terrain, or when you have to break camp and set out into unknown territory. But there are many long periods when you are walking on your path and the sun is shining. Then you are not stumbling around in fear and trembling, but walking quite comfortably and confidently. No, fear is not the overriding experience of the desert.

There is hunger and thirst in the desert, but hunger and thirst is not the normal daily experience. The Lord knows that we must eat. What he teaches in the desert is that you cannot travel very well on a full stomach. In the beginning, you frantically overeat as a compensation for all the other material props you have left behind. Little by little, the Lord educates you. You experience that the less you eat, the better you can travel. Fasting allows his presence to penetrate and sharpens your mind to see his light. You begin to feed on his presence, and, as with Jesus, God's will becomes your food.

Sometimes, to test you, the food supplies run thin. You fast, and your sense of his presence withdraws. Then there is real famine and real thirst. But not all the time. No, famine and thirst are not the ordinary occurrences of the desert.

There are evil spirits in the desert, but evil spirits do not meet you at every turn in the road. Because of the silence and the fasting and the confrontation with spiritual forces, you become better and better at recognizing what proceeds from your own heart and what proceeds from evil spirits. Sometimes, the Lord sends people to you who are struggling with evil spirits, and you must help them. The effects of these struggles remain with you, experiences both of the power of evil and the victory of Christ over all principalities and rulers of this world. In the desert you realize indeed that your struggles are not simply against flesh and blood. Yes, there are evil spirits in the desert, but your combat with them is not the predominant experience of the desert.

There are many doubts that bombard you in the desert. You wonder if you are really moving *towards* him, or if you simply are wandering around in circles. Are you moving *across* the wilderness, or are you really *lost,* not going anywhere? You wonder if you really are engaged in the search for life, or escaping from life? Are you on a search for meaning, or simply on a meaningless search? Are you really in the desert to help others—is there any real connection between your search and their salvation—or are you in a comfortable nest away from the struggles of life? Are you wasting your life or fulfilling it? Are you seeing a desert mirage, or is it a true vision? And are the voices you hear calling you to give up and come out from God or the devil, or your own weakness, or your own strength? Oh yes, there are innumerable doubts in the desert, but such doubts are not the normal state of soul.

Nor is the desert a paradise free from the things everyone else experiences. In the desert there is sin and temptation, lack of trust in God, and cowardice, laziness and self-indulgence. Most of the time they are not unusual or out of the ordinary. But these experiences are not the main focus of the desert.

What I wish to witness to very emphatically is that the center of my own desert experience has been the presence of a Companion who has taken away my radical loneliness. I meet my Creator and my Saviour in the wilderness. I meet my God, the Spouse of my heart. I meet the Being who gives all life and from whose creative hand I issued forth—to whose heart I hope to return.

I meet Jesus who died for my sins and who loves me. I speak with him every day, heart to heart. He knows my hopes and fears and dreams, and now I know I never have been and never will be completely alone.

I meet the Holy Spirit, and He guides me along the pathways of the desert, if I but desire ever so slightly to hear his voice every day. It is in the desert where I have made the fundamental transition from beautiful thoughts *about* God to the actual experience *of* God.

I meditate sometimes about having been in my mother's womb. There, completely helpless, I was fashioned little by little by some immense Power and Creative Force. It wasn't me; it wasn't my mother. Who was it, then? Of course, I don't have any conscious remembrance of being totally dependent upon the Lord.

Then I "grew up," learning how to depend on many other things besides God. In the desert, however, there is a return to dependence. Voluntarily you let go of supports – companions, material things, everything that "earth" means. And as you do so, the sense of God's presence begins to seep back into your bones and the center of your heart. You are again alone and helpless – and yet you stand, you keep walking. Who is holding you up, keeping you from disintegrating? God.

We have wonderful meditations about the marriage contract God has made with his people and with each person individually. "I will espouse you to me in love." "He who is your Creator has become your husband." Beautiful concepts and imagery! But it is only in the desert where the embrace of the Spouse can actually be experienced.

Our God is jealous. We love so many other things besides him. Purity of heart is required, and it is acquired in the loneliness and scorching heat of the desert journey. No one can keep walking unless the love of God — love of the Spouse — is the driving force. As other loves are burned away, the actual experience of God, the embrace of the Spouse, begins to be felt around the heart. We let go of other loves, yet we experience that we are tremendously loved. Who is loving us? The God who has called us into the wilderness to speak words of love to our hearts.

In the desert we are driven to discover our origin, and as we journey, we discover a most amazing and comforting fact: all the fears we had of God are not fears of *God* at all! They are really the reverse side of our false loves. We fear losing our false securities. But the desert-dweller discovers that as we let go of these false securities, fear of God's presence lessens. Our deepest mind, illuminated by faith, begins to work: "Of course, how can I possibly fear the Source of my life, the Being who made me? If I fear *him*, then literally there is no place to go in the whole universe."

In the desert I discovered that it's life-giving to face God's presence. We do not have to be afraid of God. God is our home, our destiny. It is all right to fall into the arms of the One who made us.

Many of us have waxed eloquent about the fatherhood of God, about his constant providence in our lives. "Behold the lilies of the field. . . ." Yes, in our minds we know that God personally and at each moment takes care of us. Beautiful concepts! It is only in the desert where this providential, caring activity of God can be experienced.

Why? Because there is nothing else in the desert. There is very little food and shelter. Yet, in some mysterious way, it is sufficient – more than sufficient. But how can less be enough? How can a little seem like a great deal? We begin to experience in our flesh that God really is the source of our life, that all the things we thought would make us happy and give us life really cannot. Because of his presence, we begin to experience the transition from being clothed and tormented with false desires, to being clothed with life-giving desires. It happens something like this.

Paul Evdokimov has a phrase which goes, "The need to have becomes the need not to have." This phrase expresses the movement of the driving Spirit in the realm of our desires.

Before we enter the desert we are driven by desires to possess material things. We believe that the more we have, the happier we shall be. A voluntary decision to enter the desert means that we have seen the falsity of that thrust. As we journey, we realize more and more that happiness indeed does not lie in possessing things. But we are still not free. We hoard a few items, just in case!

But if we keep walking, at some point in the desert, the Spirit will try to drive us into the country of the heart where a desire "not to have" begins to take over. Then, some voice from deep within us will cry out frantically, "Don't enter that country! You will be absolutely destitute then! You will lose everything, everything!" At that juncture we will have to make a decision about how far into the desert and into God's presence we desire to go.

Before we enter the desert we believe that having power and control over others will make us happy. The decision to enter the desert means that we have at least learned how empty power is as a means to peace. And, as we learn in the desert to lean on God's presence, *his power* trickles into our spiritual muscles.

Still, we are only beginners. We retain a certain amount of control over ourselves. We still engage in a certain amount of manipulation over others. We still are not sure if God is sufficient for us.

At some crossroads in our journey, the Spirit will seek to drive us into a seemingly powerless desert space. Then some voice from out of our very depths will shout, "Don't let go of everything! You will be utterly powerless then and fall into the void!" At this point a decision will have to be made about how far we will allow ourselves to fall into the arms of the Lord.

We were born to live! Everything in us cries out for abundant life. Before we enter the desert we seek life in endless blind alleys and dead-end streets. The decision to enter the desert means that we have decided true life transcends all limited human goods. As we travel in the desert, the passingness of everything begins to dawn on us. Inwardly we weep a little, because the earth really is beautiful. It's the only home we've ever known. But death becomes more and more obvious, more inescapable. We know that someday we must step off this earth. The Spirit tries to prepare us for this moment.

Sometime during our desert journey the Holy Spirit will say to us, "Now, step off the earth. It is passing away." Then, from the depths of our humanity, our earthiness, will come a tearful cry, "Don't let go of life! You were made to live here forever! After death there really isn't anything! Don't abandon the earth!"

At such a stage we will be asked whether we are going to fight death until our last breath, or receive it in companionship with the Lord. The desert is the only place where we can experience this transition from false to true desires. In the desert we come to understand that all the desires which tormented us and which led us astray can be transformed into life-giving energies driving us towards communion with God.

The desire for material things can be transformed into a desire to depend on God. The manipulation of reality can be transmuted into a belief in the power of truth and goodness. The fear of death can be changed into a desire to see the Beloved.

Every once in a while, on my own desert journey, I find myself on a rise overlooking a vast, dark, and unknown stretch of terrain. It is quite foreboding. Sometimes, it has taken me years — literally years! — to obtain from the Lord enough trust and courage to start down the other side of that hill. These "unknown lands" are the deeper realizations of the infinite distance between me and the Lord, a distance that, mysteriously, we are called upon to try and close, and which in a still more mysterious way already has been closed by Christ.

The descent from these rises is indeed fearful and confusing. I would be the last to minimize the struggle. But I witness to you that if we have the courage to start across these newly revealed expanses of land, the Lord very quickly comes alongside us. Thus a cycle develops: a new horizon, hesitation and fear, courage to enter, the experience of his presence. A period of peace follows until a new expanse of territory appears on the horizon again. But there has been no place where his presence has been absent. The Lord has said, "I will always be with you." And he is faithful to his promise.

Priests are compulsive preachers, ordained as they are to preach the gospel. May I end this chapter with a little preaching?

God is in the desert. Don't be afraid to enter there. God is in the desert. This interior journey is the most exciting of all journeys, the adventure of all adventures. You'll never know what real life is unless you've traveled the interior desert. God is in the desert. Don't spend too much time in the blind alleys and the dead-end streets. We all pass through them, but don't tarry there. Hurry into the desert. Whenever you arrive it will be too late. "Too late have I loved you, God. Too long have I feared to enter upon my desert journey with you. I didn't trust that you would be traveling with me—that you would be there!"

Yes, there is famine and heat and doubt and devils and darkness and fatigue and sin and temptation and meaninglessness in the desert. But those things are not what the desert is all about. God himself is in the desert. He created you, he loves you, and he waits in the desert to embrace you and lead you home.

The experiences of God in the charismatic movement are real and genuine. But at a certain point, one wishes to taste a deeper intimacy. It's as if you were at a party with a group of people. In the course of the conversation you discover a special affinity with a certain person and you say, "Let's go over there where we can talk more privately together." The joyful, communal experience of God in the charismatic movement has whetted peoples' spiritual appetites for the living God. In our spiritual ears we are hearing the invitation to enter more deeply into the desert of our hearts. I believe many post-charismatics are embarking upon deeper levels of this journey. Have courage! God is waiting for you there! He is preparing his people for a new phase of his work in the world.

Five

Love Beyond Everything

The desert, as I am using the term, is not a physical place, but the interior journey of the person to God. It is the search for Absolute Love. The deeper demands of *life together* is part of this desert. We have no idea, really, of the demands of love, until we start across the desert in earnest.

I have also been using the phrase "mysticism beyond the charisms," and am trying to expand on its meaning in a variety of ways. For me, it certainly does not mean abandonment of the use of the charisms so that one never exercises them again. What I mean is that one can be called by the Spirit into ways which de-emphasize the use of the charisms which may even prevent their expression altogether.

Because this can and does happen, and many people must live in such situations, the expression, use, and role of the charisms in the Christian life can never be the be-all and end-all of Christian existence to the point where communities and families break up over them. A charismatic spirituality is not the ultimate to which everything else should be sacrificed. Love is the ultimate. St. Paul is very clear about that. In post-charismatic situations, love may even demand the non-expression of the gifts, at least in certain stylized forms.

Very early in the charismatic movement Father Kilian McDonnell warned us about "pentecostalizing the gifts." By that he meant that the gifts can take on a variety of forms. There are many ways of speaking the Lord's word to one another besides saying, "Thus says the Lord" at prayer meetings. There are other ways of delivering people from evil spirits besides the pentecostal-style deliverance session.

I think this is what is happening now on a large scale. Post-charismatics are being shown by the Spirit how to "de-pentacostalize the gifts" to enable them to live the life of love in keeping with their personal spiritual journeys. I'm addressing myself to the fact that new situations in which post-charismatics find themselves may demand that they relinquish the expression of their gifts, either totally or partially, or that they seek new forms of expression. *This instinct comes precisely from the deeper demands of love, and therefore from the Spirit.* This instinct flows from a deeper appreciation of the fruits of the Spirit and the cost of these fruits.

What if you find yourself in a situation where your gifts are not understood, or appreciated, or even believed in? What does one do? Leave? Pout? Get angry at God? Forget about the gifts? Perhaps a few years ago, some of these solutions were tried. Now, more people are being led to a deeper kind of love. They are staying where they are, because that's where the people they love are, the people to whom they have dedicated their lives. The Spirit is teaching us deeper aspects of love, the high cost of living together, and something of what it cost Jesus to live in Nazareth.

There is a life of love, a mysticism beyond the charisms. One has to understand that love is possible without the expression of the gifts in stylized forms. Jesus in Nazareth possessed the fullness of the gifts, yet, it seems he didn't express them there at all. "Is not this Jesus, the carpenter's son? Where did he get all this?" (Mk. 6:2-3)

This is not a pious meditation on the hidden life of Jesus. We are dealing with an absolute fact of Jesus' existence among us, something which is at the heart of his kenosis, his self-emptying. God in a small hick town! How was it possible? Didn't he have to compromise a lot with his principles? Wasn't he burying his talents all those years? All that power to heal and cast out demons, and he didn't use it! He had the wisdom to change hearts, and what did he talk about with the villagers all those years? The weather?!

In order to be God in Nazareth he had to be living a kind of love that was genuine, true, and authentic. Jesus could never compromise about love. Yet, he did not use his charismatic gifts. What factors, what reasons motivated such a hidden existence? Why did he wait so long? Perhaps in order to teach us some profound and difficult truths about the cost of living together. For love of us, Jesus gave up more than we can ever understand or imagine. What follows is a meditation on the cost of this love. I truly believe that post-charismatics are appreciating this cost in a new depth and are now living out the kenosis of

Christ in more hidden but more powerful ways.

Meditating in Nazareth these past few years on the high cost of living together, three texts keep coming to me: "I pray . . . that all may be one, as you, Father, are in me, and I in you" (Jn 17:21); "Let Christ Jesus be your example as to what your attitude should be, who, though from the beginning he had the nature of God, did not cling to his prerogatives as God's equal" (Phil 2:5-6); "The way that we came to understand love was that he laid down his life for us; we too must lay down our lives for our brothers" (1 Jn 3:16). I would like to develop some of the implications of these texts for the demands of Christian love.

Christians believe in promises. We believe they form an essential part of human existence. We believe in making them, and we believe, with God's help, it is possible to keep them. The very framework of our relationship with God – the Covenant – is based on the principle of mutual commitment.

By the gospel, we are called to lay down our lives, if necessary, for anyone, to go to the ultimate demands of love for the person next to us. But to some people we are especially bound, either by natural ties of family or marriage, or commitments of a religious nature. We are called to be faithful in loving these people.

Now, let's not kid ourselves. Love is the hardest, the most difficult achievement of all. Dostoevski said that love in reality is a harsh and dreadful thing. It is not only that, but eventually it comes to real pain. Anyone who doesn't think so, doesn't really know what love is, hasn't even begun to seek true love.

Every other achievement is easier than to grow in love for other people. Writing books, getting to the moon, healing the multitudes, leading armies—you name it!—all pale into insignificance in comparison with love. Our experience tells us this. This unity in love is both the deepest cry of our hearts and what we avoid at all cost, because it costs everything! Our minds and our hearts are constantly engaged in a search for excuses and rationalizations to avoid paying the demands of love. True love is incredibly hard to achieve. It cost Jesus his life.

Because it is terribly difficult, we easily rationalize our way out of commitments. It doesn't take much to start us off on other expeditions and enterprises. In our families and communities, we rationalize that, really, there are more important things than unity and love, things that take precedence.

There is the gospel. "These people are not living the gospel, and the gospel is the most important thing. I cannot live the gospel here, so I must leave."

God's will. "God himself is calling me away from striving any longer for unity. I have done the best I can. It is God's will that I leave."

Truth. "God does not want untruth, and the truth is being compromised here. I can no longer live with untruth."

The gifts of the Spirit. "These gifts are of the essence of the Christian life. I cannot freely exercise them here. Surely God does not want me to continue in such a situation."

Now, we think like this, because we do not understand the depth of the kenosis, the self-emptying, of Christ. We do not understand his approach to unity. We do not understand that unity is more important than anything else. "What! Unity at the expense of truth! Unity at the expense of the gospel! False unity?"

Let me begin with an example.

Shortly after President Carter's election there was a bit of a scandal brewing over his church affiliation in Plains, Ga. It was discovered that the Baptist Church he attended was discriminating against blacks. How could the President of the United States belong to such a congregation! When asked about it, he simply said: "I don't agree with this policy, but it seems to me that one should stay and try to work together towards goals and not leave because one disagrees," or words to that effect. The President of the United States could belong to a segregated church just as Jesus could belong to a religion which included the Pharisees and a town whose members were capable of throwing people over cliffs!

Most often, our reasons for leaving relationships to which we have committed ourselves are rationalizations to avoid the harsh demands of love. The gospel solution is to stay together and try to work towards unity with faith in the power of Christ. Very often a change of commitment is a denial of the cross of Christ. That is the point I wish to make. I think post-charismatics are returning to their Nazareths, living and accepting on a deeper level their commitments in love.

Jesus came to unite all humankind. To accomplish this he did not cling to his prerogatives as God's equal. What was the cost of unity for Jesus?

In some sense, it cost him his divinity. He emptied himself, let go of status and power and authority and influence. He bowed down as low as he could, so that he could raise us up with him.

He lived among us! Need we say more! The Wheat of God grew among the tares. Wisdom dwelt with blindness. Love flourished alongside selfishness. Faith walked up and down the rows of unbelief. Zeal for the Father mingled with our puny little plans and our egocentric concerns. The Wheat of God didn't leave for another field. Neither did he destroy the tares. He didn't quench the smouldering flax, nor injure the bruised reed. He *stayed with us! He stuck it out!*

By joining himself to the human race, by becoming a member of the Jewish people, by living in Nazareth, Jesus inserted himself into all kinds of imperfect situations. He had come to effect unity among his people, so he was not scandalized when he didn't find it. He had promised to become one of us, so he would stick it out. He would pray with us, love us, criticize us, teach us – but he would never leave us. Even when we killed him, he came back! He had come to unite us, and he couldn't do that by giving up on us. He could only accomplish his work of unity by staying within the bosom of our race and struggling with us.

This is an extremely important point. Had Christians heeded it more in their disputes down through the centuries, it might have prevented divisions. There might have been more redemptive pain, but unity might have prevailed. It is really the parable of the wheat and the tares.

Within any individual or any group of people there is a field of tares and wheat growing – in you, in me, in all of us. When conflict arises, those who think they are the "wheat" either try to root out the "tares," or give up and move to another field. Of course, everybody thinks *they* are the wheat, and "the others" are the tares. The first mistake is making such a judgment. "Do not judge before the time," says St. Paul.

It seems to me that the Lord's own approach, both by his teaching and example, to this problem is the most demanding and crucifying of all. His command was, "Let everything grow until the harvest." Then, at harvest time, the sorting will take place. Who knows what the sorting will be like? Who will be the tares and who the wheat? If the growing together is given a chance – if there is a mutual striving towards unity – maybe the whole field in time would produce a harvest beyond anyone's expectations!

We too easily break off our efforts at unity, because unity is the most crucifying task of all. We have not understood or entered into the mystery of the kenosis of Christ in Nazareth and as a member of the human race. "He did not cling to his prerogatives as God's equal." He did not leave Nazareth when he was twenty-one because nobody appreciated his talents or his ideas! He did not repudiate the religion of his fathers even though the control of much of it was in the hands of hypocrites.

We, in our relationships, cling to our pride, our own ideas, our dreams, our sensitivities. Is "our way" of living the gospel really the way? Will I discover my maturity by seeking a group which thinks the way I think? Will I discover love by avoiding the demands of love?

Don't we understand that the sublime goal of unity may cost us the modification of all our wonderful plans? Don't we realize that if we live in the faith of the Son of God who loved us and died for us, he will bless us with true unity and love? Will any of us ever be asked to give up more than Jesus gave up?

What is the cost of unity of hearts? The cost is everything! The cost is having your heart broken like Jesus' heart was broken – and that not once but over and over again. The cost is having your "divinity" go unrecognized and even disregarded. The cost is a crucifixion of your mind and of your own small ideas about how you are going to get to God (as if you could map it out for yourself!). The cost is reaching for the thousandth time towards somebody, hoping that one day that person will reach out towards you. Everybody wants the perfection of life together, but few people are willing to give up everything for it.

In a meeting with Catherine Doherty a few years ago, she spoke about the cost of love. She got down on the floor and began to crawl slowly on her stomach towards one of the people present. Then, as she neared the person, she haltingly stretched out her hand in friendship. "That," she said, "is what it costs."

It seems to me that when we break off efforts towards love, we are admitting that Jesus is not powerful enough to create unity and love. Don't we profess that the Good News is precisely this: the power of love has entered the world in the

Person of Jesus, and that true love now is possible? True love is the only real miracle. To accept Jesus as Saviour is to believe in his power to unite people in love. This is what all the world is seeking. This is what all the songs and poetry are about. This is the miracle to which every Christian body should be witnessing. This is THE SIGN that Jesus really is from God (Jn. 17:21). To leave is to admit that love is not possible – not possible here, with this person, or with these people, in this situation. It is to say, really, that Jesus is not powerful enough to save, to heal, or to create love amidst our brokenness.

How far should you go in such a painful struggle? How far did Jesus go? Even when members of his own town sought to kill him, he did not reject his people. Rather, "He laid down his life for us." Laying down your life for the brethren does not simply mean putting up with people you dislike. It does not simply mean relinquishing opportunities for your "growth." It does not simply mean holding back your anger once in a while "to keep peace."

Laying down our lives for one another means accepting the possibility of some kind of death rather than refusing efforts towards love and concern. It means having your heart broken, feeling that you may die – but experiencing that you don't! It means risking the underdevelopment of whole areas of your life, trusting all the while that true love does not depend on such development. It means letting go, on many levels, of this value and that enrichment, hoping that by so doing Jesus will be faithful to his promises and fill you with the essence of all values and all riches – himself.

I feel too many people are giving up the struggle for love, because they have a poor understanding of what the kenosis of Christ really means and demands. We will go just so far and no further. "Beyond that," we say to ourselves, "it doesn't make sense." Does the Incarnation make sense? Does the life in Nazareth make sense? Does the Crucifixion make sense? Does Jesus' letting go of his divinity make sense?

But, after all, it is not all death and dying! When people are willing to enter into the kenosis of Jesus, when they are willing to let go of their little divinities and have their hearts broken open, then, out of that breaking issues forth what all the world is seeking – real love. This is the living water. It is Jesus. Anyone who has ever tasted him knows that he is worth everything. When true love is present – God's love – nothing else really matters. Then our maturity and our development and our emotional needs and our great ideas are all put into their proper place. From this breaking open of our heart issues forth a clear, sweet, and delicious love. A cry goes up: "The Bridegroom is here!"

Alas, so many people never really taste Jesus, because they do not really believe he is worth everything, or, if they believe it, they are not willing to pay the price. They are seeking him on superficial levels of their being, with superficial efforts, and consequently with superficial results. The love of Jesus can really be tasted only

by entering into the mystery of his very own kenosis for us.

As we wander over the face of the earth,
whether we know it or not, what we are really
seeking is a place, a family, a home where we can
taste true love. Little do most of us realize that
Love is present – was always present – right
where we are, in Nazareth. The cost of this love?
Laying down our lives for one another as he laid
down his life for us.

I believe the charismatic movement has given
people new strength to do precisely this. They
are slowly walking back to their homes and offices and neighborhoods. Equipped with new
power in the Spirit, they are now able to love better the people closest to them. People are realizing more their first responsibilities and returning
to Nazareth.

It may be a husband or wife who is difficult to
live with. An ailing mother or father. Lack of
Christian support in their social surroundings. It
is not easy. Several years ago they might not have
been able to live there with the love of Christ in
their hearts. Now they have the power of the
Spirit within them. They can discern better, and
combat more effectively, the forces around them
which they must avoid. They have returned to
Nazareth.

In early stages of people's involvement in the
charismatic movement, many rifts, misunder-
standings, tensions occurred over charismatic activity in one form or another. A husband was attracted to the renewal and the wife was not.
Tension. People were more preoccupied with the

prayer group than with the parish. Tension. Within prayer groups, there was disagreement over the nature and use of the gifts. Tension. Charismatics "came on strong" at home and in their social relationships. Tension. The list could easily be extended.

I think many of these people who were involved in stress situations over their new life in Christ have been led by the Spirit to a deeper level of that life, a deeper level of love. More secure now in their new life, they can, for love's sake, let go of some of the outward forms of the gifts and work quietly and prayerfully in building up their ordinary relationships. They have returned to Nazareth.

All these people, at one time or another, were perhaps seeking God somewhere else. Now they have discovered God in Nazareth. Now they can be at home in a deeper way. They may or may not be able to exercise the gifts. In one sense, it doesn't matter. They carry a new power around within them which radiates and penetrates their situations. They feel less that they have to make things happen, than that God is at work, quietly and simply, changing hearts through a kind of spiritual radiation.

Our Lord was saving the world in Nazareth, but in a different way. Perfectly united to the Father, love radiated from his carpenter shop into the neighborhood, the town, the country, and the whole universe. I think this is what is happening now to and through post-charismatics. They are living in their Nazareths in a deeper way than ever before. They know more clearly the price of love and unity there and are more willing and able to enter into the kenosis of Christ.

The power that is and will continue to issue forth from this second enlightenment, this further journey into the Father's heart, will be immense and will not be able to be charted, graphed, or drawn up into statistics. Much of it will remain hidden, as in Nazareth. But the world will be transformed by these deaths. There will be thousands of islands of peace and love scattered all throughout God's broken world. This is part of the "rising wave" of the renewal, and I believe it is taking place on a scale larger than we shall ever realize on earth.

Six

Winning the World for Christ

Before Jesus left Nazareth he had a clear and definite awareness of the tremendous combat that was before him. He knew that the reign of his Father was diametrically opposed to much of what was going on in the world. He knew that his uncompromising preaching of his Father's will would, sooner or later, end in a violent encounter. The forces of darkness really *are* opposed to the forces of light. It is not simply a matter of clearing up a misunderstanding and informing everyone of the gospel of love. There are forces of evil in the world which have taken up positions diametrically opposed to God. Jesus' mission was to expose and confront these forces, and to conquer them. He knew what it would cost.

Early years of involvement in the charismatic movement can be quite joyful and exciting. There is the pain involved in giving up old ways, but, generally, it is an enthusiastic time. Often, however, there is little understanding and appreciation of the ultimate consequences of our choice in following the Lord Jesus. Yes, he promises us light and life and joy, and this is certainly true.

Only gradually does it dawn on us that we also are engaged in his own confrontation with real evil. Only gradually does it dawn on us that we are not prepared to suffer according to the Spirit of the gospel.

I think many people now are realizing the cost of following the Lord in the social and political arenas. Some of these people are returning to Nazareth—not to avoid the cross, but in order to enter more deeply into prayer, fasting, love, and reflection, so that they will be able to follow Jesus all the way to Jerusalem. That journey is not easy. The cup that the Lord had to drink is very painful. People are preparing to turn their faces towards Jerusalem, but first they need some deeper nourishment, deeper instruction. Like the apostles, we want to assist the Lord in restoring the kingdom. In our modern parlance, we often call it "Winning the World For Christ." But are we ready to drink the cup with Jesus, and by "winning" do we mean the same thing Jesus means? What follows is a meditation on what winning means for the Christian.

As Christians, we believe that Jesus won life for us by hanging on a cross as a criminal. The Holy Spirit is striving mightily in us to transform that often tenuous, hesitating, and uncomprehending belief into a living faith which knows from the heart that the cross is really life-giving.

If you put together a thousand football stadiums filled with people, all shouting at winning the Super-Bowl, it would not even approach the roar of victory which ascends in heaven before the Lamb who was slain, and who now lives forever. In the *Exultet*, the great prayer of the Easter

Vigil, one of the first phrases sung on the holy night is, "Christ has conquered!" In this chapter I would like to explore this aspect of our faith, Jesus' winning the world through his cross, from a consideration of the human drive to win.

Peter Berger wrote a famous book called *A Rumor of Angels.* The "angels" were attitudes, traits, characteristics of the human personality by which we were able to transcend ourselves and our situations. There is a greatness in us which cannot be squelched by circumstances. With humor, for example, we can transcend painful occurrences: the human person can laugh in the face of tragedy and dance in the midst of the storm. These are traces in us of the divine.

I really don't remember if "winning" was one of the angels, but I think it is one. I believe the desire to win is one of the good longings and strivings and drives in us, stemming from the divine image deep down. Yes, sin, the false self, the "world" distort this drive, as many other good instincts in us are distorted. The desire to win can come from pride and domination and arrogance. But, for all that, is wanting to win wrong?

Do we not all want to win? Is not the whole point of all our games and contests, precisely, to have a winner? Nor is our experience simply one of just crushing our opponents out of malice and/or pride. Yes, I know there are modern gamesters who have devised games where nobody wins, where the goal of the game is simply to have fun together, or to foster a sense of cooperation. That's okay—to have fun together, to foster a spirit of cooperation. No doubt, many of our professional athletes could profit from such games once in a while!

But is this longing to win, to be victor, to excel in intelligence, skill, art – is this desire all bad, stemming entirely from a goal-oriented, achievement-oriented society? Is not this desire to win something from God?

From a social point of view, what a tremendous joy, sense of community, and happiness is unleashed when, upon the success of the home team, an explosion of victory cascades through several hundred thousand people in a stadium! For all its mixture with pride and sin, there is still, at bottom, something magnificent about that experience. It unites people of all ages and backgrounds, sends a sense of accomplishment and legitimate pride coursing through people. Is not this a rumor of angels?

Now I ask the rather obvious question: *Why* do we want to win? Let's abstract for a moment from the sinful aspects of the actual situations and ask: What is the essence of the rumor of angels in winning?

It is frequently noted today that the essence of spirit is its quality of self-transcendence: we can go *beyond* ourselves. With our minds we can see ourselves, conceive new goals and ideals, work towards them and acccomplish them. I think "winning" is one of the incarnations of our self-transcendence. It is a drive to go beyond where we are – in sports, in art, in contests of every imaginable kind. To do this we pit ourselves against most worthy opponents – other self-transcending beings like ourselves – who, if we can "beat" them, afford us one of the most exhilarating experiences of human nature.

This drive to win, then, stems from the essence of spirit in us. There is a greatness deep down which knows that it has untapped abilities and resources. There is, consequently, a profound desire to unleash these abilities, to explore them, to match them against others. Aquinas said that the soul is *quasi infinita,* almost infinite. In a real sense, there is no end to our abilities; they are unlimited.

Who could possibly list the number and variety of contests in the world each year, from butterfly collections to the Olympics? Art contests, square-dancing contests, beauty contests — are these not ways in which we compete in order to excel?

Even when we refuse to play games or engage in contests, we sometimes justify this with a superior attitude of seeing sports or competition as beneath us, or of not wishing to indulge in such antagonistic behaviour. But, after all, are not these attitudes just another way of winning; we have excelled all these lesser folk in our superior attitudes and stances towards life! Vince Lombardi said it (not judging how he meant it!): "Winning is not the most important thing; it's the ONLY THING!" And really, isn't it? We all want to win.

Winning is one of the images the Book of Revelation uses to describe our final salvation: "I will see to it that the victor eats from the tree of life which grows in the garden of God" (Rv 2:7); "The victor shall never be harmed by the second death" (vs. 11); "To the victor I will give the hidden manna" (vs. 17); "To the one who wins the victory, who keeps to my ways till the end, I will give authority over the nations" (vs. 26); "The victor shall go clothed in white" (Rv. 3:5); "I will make the victor a pillar in the temple of my God and he shall never leave it" (vs. 12); "Here I stand, knocking at the door. If anyone hears me calling and opens the door, I will enter his house and have supper with him, and he with me. I will give the victor the right to sit with me on my throne, as I myself won the victory and took my seat beside my Father on his throne" (vs. 20-21). In this last passage, the Lord says that he himself has won. The early Church never ceased to make this victory known with the cry, "CHRISTUS VICTOR!"

We commonly speak of the game of life. It's true. In a thousand and one ways we are trying to excel one another. The tragedy is that the true rules of the game of life are often unknown or, if known, disregarded. The rules are love and mercy and justice and kindness and truth and all the directives the Lord Jesus gave us to live by. Because many people do not know or live by these rules, the game we are playing often turns ugly. Let me use an analogy.

A hockey game is in progress. Suddenly, instead of playing by the rules and excelling one another in legitimate ways, somebody starts tripping. Somebody else trips back. Punching follows. Finally, the gloves come off and what takes place is one of those really disgusting free-for-alls you see on the ice. What was once an ennobling striving for mastery in skill becomes a contest of who can be stronger, meaner, more ruthless. The real game is over. The sinful self then strives to win at *any* cost, in *any* possible way.

This is what our wars, our interpersonal battles, our dirty business deals are, "victories at any cost." The divine drive in us to excel, to stretch our capacities, to rival one another, is perverted and focused on a new game with new rules. The rules are power, trickery and falsehood.

So Who comes to our earth? The Victor, the Master Player, the Best. Jesus came to play the game of life, the game of mercy, compassion and love. But we refused to play it his way. Maybe we never knew the rules. He tried to teach us. We didn't want to learn. We challenged him to play *our* game. "Come on, match power for power!" Jesus refused. "Come on, match hatred for hatred!" Jesus refused. "Come on, match lie for lie!" Jesus refused.

Well, in the face of such refusals, Jesus looked like a sissy. Not so. Out of his own free and enlightened will, he chose not to play our perverse little games. He chose not to contend, not to "win," since winning in our game was not ennobling, not connected at all with that spark of desire for true victory which the Father had placed in the human heart.

So they came with clubs and swords against him. He refused to call his legions of angels to demolish them. They dragged him along to the high priest. He went meekly and didn't shove back. They slapped his face. He responded with the truth. They put a purple robe on him and mocked him. He hid his regal origin. They falsely accused him. The witness of his whole life was his answer. They beat him with cords. He did not, on this occasion, make a whip of his own. They spit in his face. He swallowed their spittle. They placed a heavy cross on his shoulders. He did not break it over their heads. They nailed him to a tree. He did not command the lightning to strike them dead. They cursed him. He forgave them. They won the game of violence. Jesus won the game of truth and love.

Many times the cross is the effort, pain, struggle involved in playing the true game of love. In the eyes of unbelievers (ourselves sometimes!) it seems madness, a cop-out. Christians can appear to be sissies and marshmallows. "Put up your dukes and fight like a man!" cries the coach of the world.

We believe we do contend like true human beings, but the rules governing our contests are different. We strive for different goals. We do not fight beating the air. We have the presence of the Spirit in us who guides us to choose the kinds of games we are going to play. We do not allow ourselves simply to react to somebody else's conception of what the game is. We *know* what the game is. We have our great Champion who has gone before us, won all the prizes, and trained us to do likewise

Too often, in politics, business, and elsewhere, we allow ourselves to get sucked into false games; then we simply find ourselves reacting to evil instead of conquering it by love. Jesus was such a Victor, such a wonderful Contender, that he chose not to encourage the game of evil in any way.

When blows came at him, he absorbed them, rolled with them. He chose a bruised face rather than a blackened heart. When he was calumniated and slandered, he chose to have his reputation destroyed rather than lose his Name as the well-Beloved of the Father. His body was striped with whips. He preferred this to a compassionate Heart lined with the least trace of rage. He was mocked as a king, but did not mock the kings of the earth, lest humankind lose forever the only real vision of true kingship.

He suffered spittle to stream down his face without allowing the least moisture of that spittle to move his heart to retaliation. He allowed the thorns to be pushed into his head without in any way allowing scorn for his mockers to dim the nobility of his mind. He suffered his hands to be helplessly nailed to the cross rather than use those hands to strike his torturers. When others used their mouths for cursing, he used his to bless.

Jesus' Heart was like a bottomless well of love which absorbed evil and transformed it without reacting to it in a sinful way. We react to evil *with evil* and thus get sucked into the wrong games. Jesus saw clearly that love is the only game – the ONLY GAME – worth winning. We settle for nasty little games ruled by pride, prestige and power, and we look forward to short-term, stupid, paltry little victories.

Jesus risked being considered a softy and a sissy in the game of the world so that he might reveal to us what true victory is. He taught us that winning might not always be possible here in this life. We might not gain a victory which is visible to the eyes or the understanding of all. We fight and fight for our short-lived victories here and now lest we be left out of the sham victory celebrations of this life.

"Run to win," said St. Paul. "If you lose . . . you will save," says Jesus. They are talking about the same game. Paul says there *is* a game and contest in which we can stretch our abilities to the utmost, where our God-given desire to achieve and contend can be expressed. It is in the game of love, mercy and compassion. Paul even speaks about a holy rivalry in this contest. We were born to strive, to run, to excel. If we don't do this in the game of love, we will unleash this desire in other nasty little games of our own making.

You want to win when you get angry at yourself or others? Turn your rage into compassion. Hard, isn't it? Yet, if you don't, you will never understand the compassion of Christ.

You want to win in the battle against falsehood and lies? Don't speak falsehood or tell lies about others when they tell them about you. Hard, isn't it? If you tell lies you will never understand what Truth endured for you, or what it is to follow him who is the Truth.

You want to win in the game of love? Pray for those who don't like you, or who even hate your guts. If you don't, you'll never know what real love is, love such as the Father's who makes his light shine on all his children.

You want to win in the game of striving for justice in the world? Don't hate those who oppress the poor and cause injustice. Hard, isn't it? If you use your own heart for hatred, you will never know what your heart is for.

The author of Hebrews, in a magnificent passage, points to Jesus our Champion and encourages us to follow him: "Let us lay aside every encumbrance of sin which clings to us and persevere in running the race which lies ahead; let us keep our eyes fixed on Jesus, who inspires and perfects our faith" (Heb 12:1b-2). This text pictures Jesus as having run the great race and captured the prize of joy which is the salvation of all the faithful.

In our liturgies we sing of the beauty of the Cross:

Joy to You, most honorable Cross of the Lord!
Through you, mankind has been relieved of the curse. You are a sign of joy indeed, and of terror to our spiritual enemies; you are the help of Christians, the glory of kings, the strength of the just, the splendor of priests, a staff of power to your people and a source of peace. Around you the angels gather in awe: you are the glory of Christ Who grants great mercy to the world.

(Feast of the Exaltation of the Precious Cross,
Byzantine Rite)

Yes, this is true. We kiss the Cross; we believe it is the source of our joy and salvation. But let us remember how and why it became so. The cross is life because Jesus knew where true victory lay. He chose to lose all the petty and mean little games we consider so important so as to win the game of love.

If we fail to become great lovers of Christ, it will probably be because we have not understood, or not had the courage to live the mystery of the Cross: victory through defeat. We just couldn't live without *some* of the lesser "victories," *some* of the petty skirmishes. When the

game got rough, we couldn't avoid a few trip-
pings, a few punches, a few elbows in the ribs.
We were so enthusiastic about winning the world
for Christ that we didn't hear too clearly what the
Spirit was whispering in our ears about the name
of the game.

After all, a Champion hanging naked on a tree,
a Victor who is nailed helpless, it is all rather
hard to understand. Yes, it is hard. But if we don't
try to understand this mystery, we will never win
the world for Christ. We will be won over by the
world!

I think post-charismatics, in their social, political, and business worlds are discovering that it
is not easy to win the world for Christ. The con-
frontations with evil can sometimes only be met
by suffering. Many situations are a "no-win" situation. On one level, evil often *does* win, as it
snuffed out the life of Jesus.

I think precisely because post-charismatics' instincts have been sharpened by the Spirit in the
charismatic movement, a kind of withdrawal —
positive in nature — is taking place. The first wave
of renewal involvement is exciting and exhilarating. Singing ". . .sound the trumpets of war, Jericho must fall" in a stadium of forty thousand people can give one a great deal of enthusiasm, but
it doesn't guarantee insight or courage in the actual battles.

Jacques Ellul, in *False Presence of the Kingdom*,
emphasizes a most important factor for a true
presence of the Christian in the world: separation. It is what I have been calling "Nazareth." It
is not a geographical separation, but a radical disengagement of the heart.

Before the presence in the world can mean anything, it has to be the presence of 'that which is not of the world.' . . . the primary action, the radical decision, is that of separation. Separation is not the ultimate, but it is indispensable. . . . If this disengagement does not take place, if the discovery is not made of the specific character of the thought and life of the Christian, then the engagement being recommended to Christians is nothing but empty pursuit of a fad.[1]

Some may misunderstand this to mean another pietistic withdrawal from the "real world." That is not what is meant. But I believe post-charismatics are in a second stage of a heart-disengagement and clarification of their relationship to the world as Christians.

Christian communities are now trying to provide this "specific character of the thought and life of Christians." But what about those who cannot, for one reason or another, live in these communities? I believe many of them have entered a quiet Nazareth "separation situation" of their own, or perhaps with a few others. There they are trying to readjust their sights and strengthen their hearts for the journey to Jerusalem.

Existing Christian communities of all kinds can help these people by offering their support, witness, and teaching. By and large, it is *in communities* where spiritualities develop. There are countless saints whose individual lives inspire us but from whom we really cannot extract guidance for our lives. Other saints have a vocation from God to provide his people with a way of holiness. During their lifetimes, people gather around such saints and a new spirituality, a new way of living the gospel, is born into the Church. These groups then serve as schools of holiness for future generations.

What are the Augustinians, Benedictines, Franciscans, Cistercians, and the Little Sisters and Brothers of Charles de Foucauld but schools of holiness inspired by the Spirit?

During the last few years the Congregation of Religious has been urging Orders to open their doors to those seeking deeper life. Where can post-charismatics go for the deeper wisdom and guidance they need? The Orders have a valuable and vital role to play here. They should have confidence that they have much to share with post-charismatics. They have a wealth of tradition and spirituality. Many religious have been living a deep life of love for years, and they have a spiritual doctrine to guide them. This is what people are now seeking.

I strongly urge that post-charismatics knock on monastery and convent and community doors, and ask those inside about prayer, contemplation, mysticism, poverty and penance. God does not leave his people without food. Our countrysides and cities are dotted with these little centers of traditional spiritual wisdom.

What we are beginning to witness again is the phenomenon of "Third Orders," although they are not being called such. Traditionally (as in the Franciscans, for example), the men were the First Order, the women the Second, and lay affiliates were the Third. Today, lay people who do not feel called to join an actual community are clustering around monasteries and centers of spiritual life, much as people in the middle ages moved close to the monastery for support. People are asking if they can become affiliates in some way so as to find support and guidance for their spiritual lives. What we may see more of in the future is this tendency of families and individuals to foster their unique growth in conjunction with a more traditional school of holiness.

I spoke with a bishop recently who told me this story. He was invited to "rap" with a group of young people from Hari Krishna. Among the criticisms they leveled at him was: "Why are your religious behind closed doors? Why aren't they preaching out in the streets like we do?" The bishop said: "Come back in twenty years, and we'll discuss the matter further." He said there was a long silence and no reply. Both knew that the religious would certainly be here in the year 2,000. Neither the young people nor the bishop were too sure about Hari Krishna.

I don't believe too many post-charismatics have given up their desire to win the whole world for Christ. Anyone who has tasted, in ever so slight a way, the power of the gospel to change hearts cannot withdraw easily. But I believe many are realizing the need for something of what those religious have behind those closed doors. Post-charismatics want to be around in the year 2,000, still enthusiastic about winning the world for Christ. What they are seeking is the way, the spirituality, the kind of mysticism that will ensure their perseverance in ever greater love.

Seven

Refocus on the Church

I believe the Spirit is drawing post-charismatics into new areas and dimensions of their Christian lives. One of these dimensions is a movement back to the Church. In early periods of involvement with the charismatic movement there is often a movement away from the structures of the Church; in the very early days many people actually left because they could not find support and understanding. The second decade of the renewal will include a movement back to the Church.

One reason for this is that the renewal has graphically revealed the basic building blocks of any community which perdures for any length of time. If any group stays together long enough, it develops exactly the same characteristics of structure from which some people fled – hierarchy, a body of doctrine, authorized teachers, traditions, and so on. People are seeing more clearly that these elements are present in the scriptures themselves. A factor, then, in the movement away from the formal renewal is some kind of reevaluation and rethinking of the nature of the Church and of one's relationship to it.

Many people were attracted to the renewal because it offered them a vibrant sense of community. They didn't formally leave their Church, but much of their nourishment came from participation in things charismatic. Because of their new life in the Spirit, I believe post-charismatics are returning to the parish, to a deeper faith relationship with their bishops and shepherds, and this also is, in a way, a return to Nazareth. More mature now in the Spirit, and having a greater appreciation of the New Testament concept of Church, they are better able to live in the parish with all its inadequacies and to help work out problems which militate against a dynamic Church life.

The charismatic movement has been saying for years that the parish is the goal of all renewals. Well, that may be what is happening. Perhaps people are becoming more aware of the needs of the parish, and are trying to do something about it. What we may have to learn from the Spirit in the eighties is *the shape of this insertion of the renewal into the parishes.* Perhaps it was conceived abstractly in terms of everyone exercising the gifts, and liturgies fully alive with prophecies and charismatic songs. The Spirit may have other ideas. He may be instructing us about the different patterns and forms this aliveness can take.

People may be going about the task of renewing the parish without the gifts of the Spirit too much in evidence. There may be a prior stage of simply loving, helping, and building up trust and relationships. This quiet and non-pushy approach may be the key to attract others to what God is doing in the charismatic movement. I think the Lord has prepared many quiet but powerful witnesses to be among his people in greater depth, as a preparatory stage to further renewal.

There is another reason for this movement back to the Church. Many traditional Church people felt that they were being pulled into theological areas which were confusing their own identity. They felt that they were going too far in some of their ecumenical activity. They were beginning to miss some of the more traditional elements of their faith which the charismatic movement does not (and perhaps ought not) provide. They have returned to the parish to drink once more at these sources. The charismatic movement has helped to bring to life *certain elements* of the Christian life. But there is so much more to our faith, especially in Roman Catholicism, which often is not present in the charismatic movement.

Then there are those who never did have any formal Church affiliation. The renewal has led them to a deeper appreciation of the nature of the Church. They are tired of belonging to undefined groups which simply pray together. After accepting Jesus and understanding his gifts, they are asking themselves, "What else is there?" They are wondering about the almost two-thousand year history of Christianity, and wondering how they, in this latter part of the twentieth century, are related to the ancient community of faith – or if this ancient community still exists. This grappling with the nature of the Church is also a return to Nazareth.

We have many young post-charismatics, for example, coming to Madonna House. Some have been in the renewal for years. They are not coming to learn about the gifts or the renewal. They are coming to learn about the *Church*. They want to know about the saints and the sacraments and Our Lady. They want to know about the desert Fathers and the Eastern rites and about bishops and sacramentals. Because they have been touched by the Spirit, they want to know everything the Spirit has taught the Church down through the centuries.

It would be "pleasant" if we could just live in some loosely organized prayer group, and love and serve one another. But this is not the Church of the New Testament. Nor does this arrangement answer the question of continuity with the apostolic community, or of how one is now related to the whole of Christian tradition. Sooner or later everyone must come to grips with these deeper questions. I think many people are now back in Nazareth, praying over and grappling with their relationship to the Church. As I said, I think the charismatic movement has given people a clearer focus on the Church—but what church, and where is it?

Let us look briefly at the basic structure of the Church of the New Testament. If people already belong to a church with this structure, these remarks are meant to encourage them. If people do not belong to a church with these elements, they are meant as a guide, to help them in their search. As a Roman Catholic, I believe that this church is the ancient community of faith, containing the fullness of God's plan for his people. I think post-charismatics are present now within this church in a new and powerful manner, vivifying its life in many ways known only to God.

The aspects of the Church I wish to focus on here concern its structural, sociological elements, rather than its deeper nature as Body of Christ, People of God, etc. Everyone who is "in Christ" belongs in some way to his Body. But the Church of the New Testament is not simply a spiritual reality with no outward form. It is and was from the beginning a recognizable society, with certain definite characteristics. This is the dimension I wish to expand upon.

There is great confusion these days concerning the nature of the Church. One of the reasons for the confusion is the deluge of evangelistic radio and TV programs, mass rallies, books, tapes and magazines about the Good News that Jesus is the Saviour of the world. In one sense, it's really quite exciting and wonderful! I'm sure St. Paul, that indefatigable preacher, would use every modern means at his disposal to preach the gospel were he alive today. And I'm sure many, many people are accepting the Lord Jesus through the instrumentality of these rallies, programs and literature. People can come to the Lord any time, any place, through the preaching of anybody. In diverse ways, then, the Good News is reaching millions of people.

However, having acknowledged and even rejoiced over this fact, it also creates a situation which has serious implications as far as the New Testament concept of Church is concerned. For example, if we ask the question, "Are all these people authorized to preach the gospel?" we may seem to be dropping a wet blanket on a wonderful work of God!

Even in Jesus' time there were people not of his immediate band who were preaching and performing miracles in his name. The apostles one day came and informed him of this: "Teacher, we saw a man using your name to expel demons and we tried to stop him because he was not of our company" (Mk 9:38-39). Jesus said to leave him alone. Evidently, in some way, this person was contributing to the fostering of the kingdom.

But when the Spirit came and formed the ancient community, some definite guidelines were given about preaching the gospel. In the New Testament concept of the Christian community, there are no unauthorized preachers. Yes, there are people like our friend in the gospel, going around preaching in Jesus' name out of enthusiasm or love or other motives, but the New Testament is clear that only authorized people really speak in the name of the Church. Even if people perform miracles in Jesus' name, it does not mean they speak in the name of the Church, or that their teaching is correct simply because they are working miracles.

Much of the evangelical preaching these days is in a fuzzy area outside the New Testament understanding of the Church. Who are these people? Who has authorized them to preach? Where do they suggest people go after accepting the Lord Jesus? Often they themselves do not belong to a Church which has the characteristics of the community of the New Testament. Nor do they often preach about the Church. The Bible is quoted profusely about salvation, about the gifts of the Spirit, about deliverance and healing, but they are often astonishingly silent about what the

New Testament has to say concerning the nature of the Church.

I think coming to grips with the true nature of the Church is a further stage of spiritual maturity for many people. What follows is meant to deepen one's appreciation of the reality of the Church.

As in our own day through the mass media, etc., so, too, in the first days of the Church, people heard about and accepted Christ through ways other than the official preaching of the Church. Paul meets Jesus as a result of a direct and dramatic revelation (Acts 9). The Ethiopian court official, reading by himself the prophet Isaiah (Acts 8:26), could serve as the patron saint of all who have come to Christ by their own quiet reading of the Scriptures. Cornelius had a direct vision of how to proceed in his search for salvation. In the following centuries also, I'm sure many people came to accept Christ through the reading of apocryphal gospels, and through the preaching of unauthorized (or even heretical) teachers.

The important question, though, is: *What was God's plan in the New Testament for each of the people mentioned above?* The plan was quite plain and unambiguous. The Spirit of God always led these people to the Church; that is, to the apostles or to people who were in faith communion with them.

Saul is told to go to Ananias, and this Ananias is in communion with Barnabas and the apostles (Acts 9:27). Cornelius is told to send for Peter himself. The Spirit tells Philip to go to the Ethiopian and explain the Scriptures; he is then baptized by Philip. I think this is an extremely important scriptural fact for our times. Many evangelists neglect this connection, or do not even seem to believe there is a Church to which people can be sent.

In the New Testament there was a definite body which was the Church, and all the teachers of this Church were authorized. Even though many wonderful things happen through the preaching of many well-intentioned people, we cannot for all that neglect the New Testament witness concerning authorization.

The first teachers were the apostles themselves: ". . .having first instructed the apostles he had chosen through the Holy Spirit" (Acts 1:2). When Judas needed replacement, "they chose . . . someone that was of our company while the Lord Jesus moved among us . . ." (Acts 1:21). When Peter says, "We are his witnesses" (Acts 2:32), he is referring to those who knew the Lord during his earthly life and who had seen him resurrected. They understood Jesus' instruction to teach (Mt 28:19-20) as directed first of all and primarily to themselves as his immediate disciples.

This was the understanding of the first Christians as well. A Jewish Christian writes: "We must attend all the more to what we have heard. Announced first by the Lord, it was confirmed by those who had heard him" (Heb 2:1), namely, the apostles. The early community devoted itself to the "instruction of the apostles" (Acts 2:42).

The apostles could not carry on this task alone, so they authorized certain people to preach the gospel with which they had been entrusted. This is clear not only from the Council of Jerusalem

(Acts 15) and the earlier sending of Barnabas to Antioch (Acts 11:22), but from the numerous references to false teachers, people who had not been authorized to teach.

"Do not be carried away by all kinds of strange teaching" (Heb 13:9). "The apostles and the presbyters, your brothers, send greetings. . . . We have heard that some of our number without any instructions *from us,* have upset you with discussions and disturbed your peace of mind . . ." (Acts 15:23). "I repeat the directions I gave you when I was on my way to Macedonia: stay on in Ephesus in order to warn certain people there against teaching false doctrines . . ." (1 Tim 1:3). "You, for your part, must remain faithful to what you have learned and believed, because you know who your teachers were" (2 Tim 3:14). In the New Testament it is clear: *not everybody was an authorized teacher.*

It was not simply a matter of Church teachers communicating falsehood, which is still a problem! It is more definite: only certain people are authorized to teach. Good will is not sufficient. There are no self-appointed teachers and preachers. We might also note that Paul knew of preachers who "traded on the Word of God" (2 Cor 2:17). We cannot discount the fact that in our day also there are still such people.

As an argument, the self-appointed teachers may liken themselves to St. Paul, which is presumptuous to say the least! Paul received his commission directly from the Lord. More than that, we are told quite clearly that Paul "stayed with the apostles" and had his doctrine checked out by them. Only then was he approved to teach the Gentiles. In another instance, Barnabas and Paul are seen to be very much an integral part of the Antiochian community. Paul is organically united with the Jerusalem Church. In the New Testament, one simply does not receive a commission to preach and teach from a private revelation or from a private understanding of the gospel.

Next, what were some of the features of this authorization?

It is clear from the Council of Jerusalem that there was in the early Church a *central authority.* "The apostles and presbyters convened to look into the matter" (Acts 15:22). Then this central body sent a letter to the churches, giving its opinions. "The apostles and the presbyters, your brothers, send greetings to the brothers of Gentile origin in Antioch, Syria, and Cilicia." "It is the decision of the Holy Spirit and ours. . . ."

It is clear from this language that these apostles and presbyters believed they were a ruling, teaching, discerning body for all the other churches. In other words, there were no autonomous communities in the New Testament as regards doctrine and practice. In important matters, the churches were regulated by a governing body outside of themselves. The Letters of the New Testament are, by and large, just such instructions from this governing body to these new communities. In short, there was an overriding teaching authority which governed all the churches.

Another characteristic of early Church preaching was that it flowed out of a wider oral tradition which was handed down along with the written word.

"Take as a model of sound teaching what you have heard me say, in faith and love in Christ Jesus. Guard the rich deposit of faith with the help of the Holy Spirit who dwells within us" (2 Tim 1:13-14). "We must attend all the more to what we have heard. . . . Announced first by the Lord, it was confirmed to us by those who had heard him" (Heb 2:1-3) "Therefore, brothers, stand firm. Hold fast to the traditions you received from us, either by our word or by letter" (2 Thes 2:15). "I feel obliged to write and encourage you to fight hard for the faith delivered once for all the saints" (Jude 3).

In the early Church, the "rich deposit of faith," the "traditions," the "faith once and for all delivered to the saints," was passed on by authorized teachers orally as well as in written form. Although the conclusion of John's gospel is an obvious literary device, does it not indicate clearly that the apostolic experience of the Lord is the wider context out of which the writings flowed? "There are still many other things that Jesus did, yet if they were written about in detail, I doubt there would be room enough in the entire world to hold the books to record them" (Jn 21:25).

The apostles communicated many things to people like Barnabas, Apollos, Timothy, Luke, Mark, Aristarchus and others, that were not written down in the gospels and letters. This means that the early Church did not simply preach "from the Scriptures." The Spirit working through them created the Scriptures. It is the Spirit teaching the community which is the prior reality. The risen

Christ is at work, guiding and teaching his Church through the Spirit, just as he promised. And this Church has very definite lines of communication for passing on this teaching.

Christians down through the centuries continued to believe in a definite tradition being handed on in this Church. In the second century, St. Irenaeus writes:

> It is within the power of all, therefore, in every Church, who may wish to see the truth, to contemplate clearly the tradition of the apostles manifested throughout the whole world; and we are in a position to reckon up those who were by the apostles instituted bishops in the Churches, and to demonstrate the succession of these men in our own times. . . .[1]

In the third century, in North Africa, Tertullian witnesses to the understanding of the Church in his own day:

> Our Lord Jesus Christ himself declared what he was, what he had been, how he was carrying out his Father's will, what obligations he demanded of men. This he did during his earthly life, either publicly to the crowds or privately to his disciples. Twelve of these he picked out to be his special companions, appointed to teach the nations.
>
> They set up churches in every city. Other churches received from them a living transplant of faith and seed of doctrine, and through this daily process of transplanting they became churches.

The only way in which we can prove what the apostles taught – that is to say, what Christ revealed to them – is through these same churches. They were founded by the apostles themselves, who first preached to them by what is called the living voice and later by means of letters.[2]

These Christians of the third century believed they were in historic continuity with the Church of the New Testament.

Jesus promised to be with his Church until the end of time. At the very least, this must have meant that his Church continued on down through the centuries with everything that was necessary to keep it true to his Name. The forces of hell were never able to destroy the essential elements of that community.

Were this not so, Jesus would have proved unable to keep his promise. There must be present, then, in the world today, the Church of the New Testament, communities of faith, living according to the New Testament model, and which can trace their origin back to this ancient Church. I believe many post-charismatics, more aware of the nature of the Church of the New Testament, are seeking to enter more deeply into this ancient community of faith.

There were other characteristics of the New Testament Church, which was really an interlocking, interconnected system of communities. It possessed a common discipline (1 Cor 11:16), interchange of personnel (1 Thes 3:2), mutual financial assistance (2 Cor 9). The early Church was a eucharistic community, celebrating weekly the Lord's supper (Acts 2:42).

123

Frequently, in evangelistic preaching and teaching, this is not the Church which is preached. What follows is a typical description of the "church" described in much current literature. The author is not important, since it is representative of what I wish to point out.

People are invited to join a "group which will fulfill your needs." The following are guidelines:

Do they honor and uplift the Lord Jesus Christ?

Do they respect the authority of Scripture?

Do they make room for the moving of the Holy Spirit?

Do they exhibit a warm and friendly attitude?

Do they seek to work out their faith in practical day to day living?

Do they build up interpersonal relationships among themselves that go beyond merely attending services?

Do they provide pastoral care that embraces all your legitimate needs?

Are they open to fellowship with other Christian groups?

Do you feel at ease and at home among them?

It is implied that if you find such a "group," you will be in a church of the New Testament.

These characteristics could easily apply to a group of people down the street who have been meeting for a month or so. It may be a nice group of people, but is it the Church of the New Testament? I think many post-charismatics are discovering that such groups cannot fulfill their long-term needs, nor answer their deeper questions about the Church and its tradition. There is a dynamic of the Spirit which seeks to plumb the depths of the traditions of Christianity, the rich deposit of faith, and the relationship between the self and the ancient community of faith.

When these questions are asked, people begin turning to more traditional structures. In early stages of enthusiasm, people are hungry for God, and are satisfied with simple evangelistic messages, and fellowship with groups of Christians. But a certain juncture is reached where these no longer satisfy, and one embarks in earnest on a search for the ancient community of faith.

Many people in the charismatic movement have no formal church affiliation. When they pass through the renewal, they seek a more traditional matrix out of which they can live their Christian faith. They too are on the road to Nazareth. They are seeking a home, the Church, their spiritual Mother, which has been in the world for two thousand years and which is waiting with open arms to welcome them home.

Afterword

It is frequently pointed out in histories of spirituality, and of religious life, that ages of crisis in the world are also the great ages of mysticism. The reasons are not hard to discover. When the world is breaking up, people seek more desperately for ultimate truth and guidance and for more than human aid in what seems a hopeless situation. God is mightily at work as well, pouring out graces in greater abundance in answer to the needs of his people.

Whatever else we are in, we are certainly in a period of crisis. All the words have been used to describe our century—transition, upheaval, new epoch, apocalyptic, etc. Who can really calculate the effects on mankind—culturally, spiritually, psychologically—of going from the horse and buggy to the moon in the course of sixty years? So we are in an age of mysticism as well, a more intense period of the longing of the human spirit for the divine.

This book is not a plea for the mysticism of Nazareth. I merely tried to describe something I see happening. The book is rather a plea for broadness of vision, a plea for the recognition of all kinds of mysticism in our times. We need all the mysticism we can get! We need mystics in the marketplace, and mystics in the caves on the mountains. We need mystics in the charismatic renewal, and mystics in the Nazareths of the world. We need everyone to seek God passionately in the variety of ways that have always been recognized and encouraged by the Church in her long experience of dealing with God-seekers.

We need to encourage one another in our individual calls. The book is a plea for reverence before the mystery of grace operative in others. It is not a matter of simply leaving everyone to do his or her own thing in the Christian life, as if we did not know definitely what being a Christian is. In the collective wisdom of the Church, we *do* know: "He who follows me does not walk in darkness."

But the Spirit not only gives people different gifts in the charismatic sense, he also calls people to different kinds of mysticism, different ways of loving, different approaches to being the presence of Christ in the world. The book will have served its purpose if it helps people broaden their vision of the creativity of God among his people.

Footnotes

Chapter 2

1. Rahner, Karl, *Theological Investigations, Volume III, Theology of the Spiritual Life*, Trans. by Karl-H, and Boniface Kruger (Baltimore: Helicon Press, 1967), pp. 87-88.

2. Rahner, Karl, *Theological Investigations, Volume XVI, Experience of the Spirit: Source of Theology.* Trans. by David Morland, O.S.B. (New York: The Seabury Press, 1979), p. 51.

3. *Ibid.*, 44.

4. *Ibid.*

5. *Ibid.*, 47.

6. *Ibid.*, 35.

7. *Investigations III*, p. 22.

8. *Investigations XVI*, pp. 47-48.

9. *Ibid.*, 10.

10. *The Spirituality of the New Testament and the Fathers,* Trans. Mary P. Ryan (London: Burns & Oates Ltd. and Desclee & Co. Inc., 1963), pp. 369-70.

11. Danielou, Jean, *Platonisme et Theologie Mystique,* (Aubier, Editions Montaigne), pp. 18-19.

12. *Ibid.,* 22-23.

13. R. Garrigou-Lagrange, O.P., *The Three Ages of the Interior Life,* Trans. Sr. M. Timothea Doyle, O.P. (St. Louis, Mo.: B. Herder Book Co., 1949), 2 Vols.

14. Wild, Robert A., *Enthusiasm in the Spirit,* (Notre Dame, Ind.: Ave Maria Press, 1975), Chapter Four.

Chapter 3

1. Ellul, Jacques, *False Presence of the Kingdom,* Trans. C. Edward Hopkin (New York: The Seabury Press, 1972), p. 85.

2. Pennington, Basil, *Centering Prayer,* (New York: Doubleday & Co. Inc., 1980), p. 204.

3. *Ibid.,* 205.

4. Doherty, Catherine, *The People of the Towel and the Water,* (Denville, N.J.: Dimension Books Inc., 1978).

5. Johnston, William, *The Inner Eye of Love,* Mysticism and Religion (San Francisco: Harper & Row, Publishers Inc., 1978), pp. 37-38.

6. *Ibid.,* 134.

Chapter 6

1. Ellul, Jacques, *False Presence of the Kingdom,* Trans. by C. Edward Hopkin (New York: The Seabury Press, 1972), p. 86.

Chapter 7

1. St. Irenaeus, *Against Heresies*
2. Tertullian, *On the Presciption of Heretics,* pp. 20-22.

Additional books from
LIVING FLAME PRESS
Order from your bookstore or
direct from Living Flame Press

FINDING PEACE IN PAIN
The Reflections of a Christian
Psychotherapist   3.50

Yvonne C. Hebert, M.A., M.F.C.C. This book offers a positive approach to overcome the paralyzing effects of emotional hurt in difficult life situations which can't be avoided or changed. Each of the ten chapters clearly illustrates how this form of special prayer can transform life's hurts into opportunities for emotional and spiritual growth. Ms. Hebert draws the reader into the real-life situations of those whom she counsels to join their pain to the sufferings of Christ in His Passion.

THIRSTING FOR GOD
IN SCRIPTURE   2.95

James McCaffrey, D.C.D. In this book, the author directs our attention to the Bible as a means of slaking that thirst, as a true source of light for the searching mind and heart. Several texts of scripture are quoted at length and discussed. The copious references from other texts, not quoted, enable the reader to compare and contrast for him/herself the ways of the Spirit. It is by reading the Bible text itself that the truth and comfort of God's word may sink into our lives.

PRAYING WITH MARY   2.95

Msgr. David E. Rosage. This handy little volume offers twenty-four short meditations or contemplations on the key events in the life of our Blessed Mother. The presentation is short, simple and to the point. The object is to turn the user to the New Testament so that he or she can bask in the light of God's Word, grow in love of that Word and respond to it as fully as possible. For a growing insight into Mary's interior life, these short reflections can be very helpful. *Reign of the Sacred Heart*

SPIRITUAL DIRECTION
Contemporary Readings   5.95

Edited by Kevin Culligan, O.C.D. The revitalized ministry of spiritual direction is one of the surest signs of renewal in today's Church. In this book seventeen leading writers and spiritual directors discuss history, meaning, demands and practice of this ministry. Readers of the book should include not just a spiritual elite, but the entire Church — men and women, clergy and laity, members of religious communities.

ENCOUNTERING THE LORD
IN DAILY LIFE   3.95

Msgr. David E. Rosage. Delightfully spiced with humor and full of wisdom, this book is intended for all who would like to follow St. Paul's admonition to "pray constantly" but who "don't have time." The author helps us turn the mundane actions of life—sipping a cup of coffee, the exhilaration of jogging or the anonymity of an elevator ride—into food for prayer. The book also has quotations from Scripture which focus on the chapter and can carry through to our daily lives.

THE RETURNING SUN
Hope for a Broken World   2.50

George A. Maloney, S.J. In this collection of meditations, the author draws on his own experiences rooted in Eastern Christianity to aid the reader to enter into the world of the "heart." It is hoped that through contemplation of this material he/she will discover the return of the inextinguishable Sun of the universe, Jesus Christ, in a new and more experiential way.

BREAD FOR THE EATING   2.95

Kelly B. Kelly. Sequel to the popular *Grains of Wheat*, this small book of words received in prayer draws the reader closer to God through the imagery of wheat being processed into bread. The author shares her love of the natural world.

LIVING HERE AND HEREAFTER
Christian Dying, Death and Resurrection   2.95

Msgr. David E. Rosage. The author offers great comfort to us by dispelling our fears and anxieties about our life after this earthly sojourn. Based on God's Word as presented in Sacred Scripture, these brief daily meditations help us understand more clearly and deeply the meaning of suffering and death.

PRAYING WITH SCRIPTURE IN THE HOLY LAND
Daily Mediations With the Risen Jesus 3.50

Msgr. David E. Rosage. Herein is offered a daily meeting with the Risen Jesus in those Holy Places which He sanctified by His human presence. Three hundred and sixty-five scripture texts are selected and blended with the pilgrimage experiences of the author, a retreat master, and well-known writer on prayer.

DISCERNMENT:
Seeking God in Every Situation   3.50

Rev. Chris Aridas. "Many Christians struggle with ways to seek, know and understand God's plan for their lives. This book is prayerful, refreshing and very practical for daily application. It is one to be read and used regularly, not just read" *(Ray Roh, O.S.B.).*

DISCOVERING PATHWAYS TO PRAYER   2.95

Msgr. David E. Rosage. Following Jesus was never meant to be dull, or worse, just duty-filled. Those who would aspire to a life of prayer and those who have already begun, will find this book amazingly thorough in its scripture-punctuated approach.

"A simple but profound book which explains the many ways and forms of prayer by which the person hungering for closer union with God may find him" *(Emmanuel Spillane, O.C.S.O., Abbot, Our Lady of the Holy Trinity Abbey, Huntsville, Utah).*

134

MOURNING:
THE HEALING JOURNEY
2.95

Rev. Kenneth J. Zanca. Comfort for those who have lost a loved one. Out of the grief suffered in the loss of both parents within two months, this young priest has written a sensitive, sympathetic yet humanly constructive book to help others who have lost loved ones. This is a book that might be given to the newly bereaved.

THE BORN-AGAIN CATHOLIC
3.95

Albert H. Boudreau. This book presents an authoritative imprimatur treatment of today's most interesting religious issue. The author, a Catholic layman, looks at Church tradition past and present and shows that the born-again experience is not only valid, but actually is Catholic Christianity at its best. The exciting experience is not only investigated, but the reader is guided into revitalizing his or her own Christian experience. The informal style, colorful personal experiences, and helpful diagrams make this book enjoyable and profitable reading.

WISDOM INSTRUCTS HER CHILDREN
The Power of the Spirit and the Word 3.50

John Randall, S.T.D. The author believes that now is God's time for "wisdom." Through the Holy Spirit, "power" has become much more accessible in the Church. Wisdom, however, lags behind and the result is imbalance and disarray. The Spirit is now seeking to pour forth a wisdom we never dreamed possible. This outpouring could lead us into a new age of Jesus Christ! This is a badly needed, most important book, not only for the Charismatic Renewal, but for the whole Church.

GRAINS OF WHEAT
2.95

Kelly B. Kelly. This little book of words received in prayer is filled with simple yet often profound leadings, exhortations and encouragement for daily living. Within the pages are insights to help one function as a Christian, day by day, minute by minute.

LIVING FLAME PRESS
Box 74, Locust Valley, N.Y. 11560

QUANTITY

_____ Post-Charismatic Experience — 4.50

_____ Finding Peace in Pain — 3.50

_____ Thirsting for God in Scripture — 2.95

_____ Praying with Mary — 2.95

_____ Journey Into Contemplation — 3.95

_____ Spiritual Direction — 5.95

_____ Encountering the Lord in Daily Life — 3.95

_____ The Returning Sun — 2.50

_____ Bread for the Eating — 2.95

_____ Living Here and Hereafter — 2.95

_____ Praying With Scripture in the
Holy Land — 3.50

_____ Discernment — 3.50

_____ Dicovering Pathways to Prayer — 2.95

_____ Mourning: The Healing Journey — 2.95

_____ The Born Again Catholic — 3.95

_____ Wisdom Instructs Her Children — 3.50

_____ Grains of Wheat — 2.95

NAME _____

ADDRESS _____

CITY _____ STATE _____ ZIP _____

Kindly include $.70 postage and handling on orders up to $5; $1.00 on
orders up to $10; more than $10 but less than $50, add 10% of total; over
$50, add 8% of total. Canadian residents add 20% exchange rate, plus
postage and handling. N.Y. State residents add 7% tax unless exempt.

8613